The Mythmakers

The Mythmakers

An Essay
On Power and Wealth

Bernard D. Nossiter

HOUGHTON MIFFLIN COMPANY BOSTON
The Riverside Press Cambridge
1964

330.973
N 897

First printing

To Jackie

Preface

I suppose I first became aware of economic problems as a boy in the early 'thirties. Playing in Central Park in New York City, I came across and wondered about the men living in shacks of wooden crates and tin cans. The Hoovervilles, of course, have vanished from the Park although some of their inhabitants' lineal descendants can still be found in the squalid side streets of the upper West Side. The problem today is much smaller, but I still have trouble seeing the sense in a world where some are compelled to be idle while most want more of the goods and services they could produce. Even stranger is the fact that economists are now more or less agreed, despite differences of emphasis, on the ways to achieve full employment and rising production. The remaining barriers are the much more formidable ones of politics, habit, institutions and culture.

Perhaps a personal preference for order and logic leads me to believe that these barriers are crumbling. To be sure, the simple faith of the eighteenth century *philosophes* in a world of increasing rationality can hardly be supported in the last half of the twentieth century. We are all children of a darker sophistication now. But of all the problems that appear to be technically obsolescent, surely that of increased material welfare in advanced industrial states must be high on the list.

Indeed, I would guess that many of the concerns of this book will be out of date in the world in which my sons are men— assuming of course that there is a world for them to live in.

Several friends, scholars and colleagues have generously read and criticized portions of the manuscript. If I have not always followed their suggestions, the fault is mine. Those who have tried to save me from error are Emile Benoit, John Blair, Otto Eckstein, Louis Hartz, James Knowles, Wassily Leontief, Sumner M. Rosen, Shelby Scates, Robert Solow and Thomas Schelling's graduate seminar in economics and national security. Richard F. Kinney, the reference librarian at the Littauer Library, and his staff put up with all manner of unreasonable demands. Mrs. Catharine Cooper compiled the back notes and checked the manuscript.

I am grateful to the Nieman Foundation for providing me with the academic year at Harvard where this book was written. Above all, I am grateful to my wife who not only typed two versions but gave me the encouragement to begin and finish this task.

B.D.N.

Washington, July 1963

Contents

The Mythmakers

I. The Corporate Vision
and the New Frontier

For the great enemy of the truth is very often not the lie—deliberate, contrived and dishonest—but the myth—persistent, persuasive and unrealistic.

—John F. Kennedy

THIS BOOK attempts to describe the anatomy and operation of the American political economy. It is concerned with identifying the principal forces at work, examining their consequences and prescribing some remedies for clear and present ills. The first two chapters are devoted to the economics of the Kennedy administration because the problems it faced and its choice of solutions illuminate themes that recur throughout this inquiry. Clearly, the Administration did not create but inherited the present structure. Whether President Kennedy attempted to preserve or change it, indeed whether change is needed are among the central questions raised here.

The term "political economy" may have an archaic sound for modern readers, having largely passed out of use in this century. But the classical economists who employed it had a fruitful insight that some of their more sophisticated (and more sterile) descendants lack. The conventional division between politics and economics is artificial. It obscures rather than illuminates any analysis of the real world. The sources and exercise of power—the concern of politics—is inextricably bound up with the distribution of limited resources among limitless uses, the concern of economics. To talk of the power of market forces, the power of unions or the power of a monopolist is to talk necessarily of a political as well as an economic structure. This book seeks to reunite two terms that have been divorced for too long. The new marriage challenges some stereotyped notions that have inhibited more rational, more productive policy making.

The most obvious link between politics and economics today appears in the policies of a President and the executive branch generally. Moreover, the very programs that an administration feels free to adopt reflect many of the underlying forces at work in the American political economy. This is another reason for beginning with a look at the economics of the Kennedy administration. This will not only serve as a springboard for our larger inquiry. It also illustrates one of the most pervasive and least useful of contemporary economic myths, the notion that the Administration challenged our business society.

*   *   *

In the early spring of 1961, Luther Hodges, the amiable Secretary of Commerce and oldest Cabinet member in the Kennedy administration, startled Washington by delivering an open challenge to the Business Advisory Council. Hodges told this corporate elite that it must abandon its secret, unsupervised meetings and open its carefully guarded ranks to some representatives of small business. This command flowed naturally out of an earlier, successful engagement that Hodges had enjoyed with the Council, or BAC, as it is known in Washington's alphabetized world. A few weeks before, he had quietly persuaded the BAC to find a new chairman.

The old chairman had been Ralph J. Cordiner, head of the General Electric Co., the firm at the center of an epic criminal antitrust conspiracy case. Hodges had carefully refrained from publicly telling the BAC that it was wrong for GE's chairman to head the leading business advisory group to the government. But asked about the awkward situation at a press conference, Hodges remarked in his euphemistic businessman's fashion: "I do not like anything of the character I saw in the newspapers."

To sensitive observers of the Capitol scene, Hodges' attempt to reform the BAC was a remarkable weather vane for the new winds sweeping Washington. Nothing of great substance was involved; nobody's fortunes were very much affected. But the sixty-three-year-old Commerce Secretary was pinching the status nerves of the business executives. And for many of the mandarins who direct corporate dynasties loss of face is more punishing than a ten point drop in the shares on which they hold options.

The little-known Business Advisory Council included in its ranks the bluest of blue chip corporate leaders. Its self-perpetuating membership of about 160, mostly corporation chairmen and presidents, embraced the two largest automobile makers; two of the Big Four in rubber; two of the Big Three in steel; two of the Big Three in chemicals and so on. It was set up in the early days of the New Deal as a conduit between powerful businessmen and the government. Nominally, the Council was an advisory group to the Commerce Department; in fact, leading officials in more important sectors of government had regularly met with the BAC at its bleak Washington gatherings or at the more relaxing work and play sessions in resorts like White Sulphur Springs, West Virginia or Pebble Beach, California. Because the Council has never published its minutes, no outsider knows how influential, if at all, the Council has been on government policy. Indeed, there is reason to believe that the BAC got more than it gave from the high federal officials who met secretly with it.

As Hobart Rowen, the Council's most perceptive chronicler

observed, the Council members at the very least got "a feel of government policy and intentions that is unique."

This special role inspired Hodges' demands for reforms. A group of business advisers to government generally, he was saying, ought to have a more representative base; should not be privy to information denied other businessmen and the public at large; and should include a public observer at their deliberations. Moreover, Hodges was saying, the advisers should not be led by the chairman of a corporation found guilty in an antitrust case.

Hodges' proposals were anomalous on two counts. The Commerce Secretary, by tradition, is supposed to represent business in the councils of government, not reform it. Moreover, there was little in Hodges' own background to suggest the iconoclast. A businessman, enthusiastic Rotarian and former Governor of North Carolina, his chief previous distinction had grown out of a bitter textile strike. His ambiguous performance in that affair had led the Textile Workers of America to accuse him of supporting a double cross.

He had earned his place in the Cabinet largely because he had led an organization designed to assure businessmen that candidate Kennedy was a fiscal conservative. Thus, in the BAC affair, the tamest tiger in the new Administration's zoo was showing his claws to the lions of the business world. And the contentious bone was an abstract question like democratic behavior. If this was a sample, the New Frontier promised to provide excitements of a large order.

Just as surprising, the Council apparently capitulated with only a few private, off-the-record mutterings. Cordiner had stepped down as BAC chairman to be replaced by Roger M. Blough, head of United States Steel Corp.; the Council agreed to have a government official present at its closed meetings, to permit newspaper reporters at all sessions addressed by government officials, to follow agendas drawn up by the Secretary of Commerce and to add some small businessmen to its membership.

A few months later, while Hodges was away salmon fishing in Canada, Blough and the Council's executive committee met with President Kennedy at the White House. The businessmen blandly told the President that they were divorcing themselves from the Commerce Department in order to "serve all areas of the government." This was corporate language for: "We don't like the new rules. We're picking up our marbles. Do you want to do anything about it?"

Blough and his fellow executives came out of the White House smiling. Press Secretary Pierre Salinger said that the President thought the reorganization "would be a good plan." The Commerce Department's acting chief in Hodges' absence, Under Secretary Edward Gudeman was not similarly enchanted. He wrote the businessmen that if they pulled out, Hodges would form a new Business Advisory Council. But in the event, the Kennedy administration swallowed the Council's counterchallenge. No new body was formed. The President went even further and invited the newly independent and renamed Business Council to make a study for him of the balance of payments. Administration officials resumed their private meetings with the closed Council group and turned to its members for help when Kennedy's 1963 tax program hit a snag.

This little episode provided an important clue to the character of the new administration (although it was overlooked in the excitement caused by Blough's later challenge on steel prices). The politically sophisticated businessman, a description that fits most Council members who regularly shuttle between their corporate citadels and the Capital, might have drawn these tentative conclusions from the clash with Hodges:

· Business had little to fear from Kennedy. He was willing to sacrifice the prestige of a lesser cabinet officer to satisfy business demands for face.

· The Administration's bark was considerably stronger than its bite. Its rhetoric should not be taken for deeds.

· Business should maintain a steady pressure on the new regime. The more business demanded, the more it was likely to get.

To be sure, Blough, perhaps reading the lesson a little too crudely, was induced to take his seemingly reckless price action the following year. But the President's inevitable response to this affront should not obscure the essential nature of the Administration's attitude towards business. The crucial domestic policies of the Kennedy regime, those affecting the control of the economic order and the distribution of the economy's abundance, were much closer in substance to contemporary corporate doctrine than most businessmen realize or will admit. A close examination of these policies will make clear that the Administration did not demonstrate any wish to tamper with the existing order; its principal difficulties with business arose over its very attempts to resolve some of the grievances voiced by businessmen.

One of the President's closest advisers once remarked that his boss was a puzzle. "I'm not sure," this aide said, "whether Kennedy is really a liberal who sometimes talks like a conservative or a conservative who sometimes uses a liberal rhetoric."

Nowadays, when at least some businessmen endorse Keynesian budget policies and at least some union leaders talk of statesmanlike restraint in collective bargaining, categories like liberal and conservative become blurred in economic affairs. There is, however, a conventional definition holding that conservative programs are those generally supported by business-

men. By this somewhat simple test, the main thrust of the
Administration's three years in office were clearly in the conservative direction. The fact that businessmen loudly denounced Kennedy policies which they themselves had previously espoused tells more about the political pathology of
corporations than it does about the Administration's economics. The triumph of the Business Council over Hodges,
then, was very much part of a pattern.

Even before this symbolic episode, the Administration
had given substantive evidence of its central drift. Kennedy
took office as the nation's fourth business slump since World
War II was reaching the bottom. In a series of dramatic press
conferences and messages to Congress, he announced an extensive catalogue of measures to reverse the tide. The fact
that the economy began moving upward again before any of
these measures took hold is cited as proof that they made no
difference; conversely, the strength of the recovery in its early
months is cited as proof that the prescription was both proper
and useful.

Apart from this argument a much more interesting question can be posed: did Kennedy's program differ materially
from that proposed by Eisenhower in similar circumstances
in the winter of 1958? The answer tells a lot about the
Administration. Stripped of inconsequentials like speedier
refunds of overpaid taxes (a step taken by Eisenhower, too),
the core of the Kennedy attack was a directive to federal
agencies to speed up their purchases under programs already
approved by Congress. Other important steps were special
stimuli for home building and home buying and a temporary
continuation of unemployment pay to jobless workers who
had exhausted their benefits. In addition, the Administration
coaxed a somewhat reluctant Federal Reserve Board to hold
down interest rates on loans of long duration, thereby encour-
aging some extra borrowing and spending.

The Administration also claimed that three other measures were major ingredients of its anti-recession recipe, but the claim is dubious. With the President's blessing, Congress finally enacted a $394 million bill to aid regions of chronic unemployment. But this had been a standard item on the Democratic legislative menu for several years and did not break new ground. The Administration also asked for and won increased social security benefits and an increase in the amount and coverage of the minimum wage. Whatever the social and humanitarian virtues of both measures, neither could properly be called anti-recession. The social security improvements provided no net increase in purchasing power because they were paid for later with higher taxes. Thus, the extra dollars received by the elderly were ultimately offset by the extra dollars given up by workers and employers. Similarly, the newly enlarged minimum wage redistributed but did not add to the total flow of incomes. In this case some businessmen gave up dollars to some workers. Indeed, in a period of comparatively high unemployment, the enlarged minimum wage probably reduced jobs by encouraging employers to lay off marginal workers.

How different was Eisenhower's approach three years earlier? He, too, relied primarily on a quickening pace of expenditures that had already been approved. He also sought and won extra jobless payments for unemployed workers. He approved a variety of measures to spur housing. And a more sympathetic Federal Reserve Board aggressively attacked interest rates on loans of short duration. As a result, the cost of borrowing for long periods fell too and even more sharply than it did during the early months of the Kennedy recovery.

Both the Eisenhower and Kennedy programs were distinguished by the fact that they came too late, that their impact was felt after the slumps they were designed to reverse had already reversed themselves. Of course, this was not Kennedy's fault; he started his term at the end of the recession. Both programs increased federal spending and this helped strengthen the recovery. The Kennedy outlays were bigger, but the difference was largely in defense spending which most businessmen regard as unobjectionable.

In sum, apart from measures that had little or nothing to do with recession, the New Frontier's program was in the main copied from Eisenhower's earlier model. Indeed, a study by Wilfred Lewis, Jr., for the Brookings Institution concludes that "the purely (or primarily) counterrecession actions" taken by Kennedy "were not vastly different from those attempted in the two previous recoveries." Since the Eisenhower administration, the chosen instrument of an important sector of business, presided over those two earlier recoveries, its approach is a good index of what most leading corporations really want or will really accept from government. And since the Kennedy and Eisenhower anti-slump attacks were similar, the Kennedy program could only give genuine concern to business leaders unable to distinguish shadow from substance.

Such conclusions pained the President's liberal supporters who wanted to claim Kennedy for their own. So they developed a kind of ritual explanation that ran along these lines:

Of course the President wanted to adopt a bolder program but he was the victim of a peculiar, inhibiting circumstance. The nation has been running a deficit in its balance of international payments. A more ambitious program would have shaken the confidence of foreign bankers, increased the run on the dollar and hastened the flow of American gold to European central banks.

The balance of payments "crisis" has generated a family of myths all its own. Since it involves international accounting, nonspecialists have been too intimidated to examine conventional financial wisdom in this area. A few simplifying observations, however, may reduce this ogre to its proper size. The famous, mysterious and inhibiting deficit is the gap between the nation's spending and earnings overseas. It has arisen largely because American dollars suddenly began flowing at an accelerated pace into foreign stocks, bonds and plants and because the United States spends heavily on military forces and installations overseas. This conclusion has been underlined in a new study by Hal B. Lary for the National Bureau of Economic Research. He calculated that foreign aid, overseas military spending and investment abroad have jumped about $3 billion annually in recent years, an amount about equal to the total deficit.*

Contrary to a popular belief, the deficit does not arise because American products are priced out of foreign markets. In fact, sales of American goods abroad are consistently larger than American purchases from foreigners. In 1961 and 1962, this *favorable* balance of trade was running nearly $5 billion annually.† But the favorable balance of trade in goods has not been big enough to close the gap created by foreign investments and defense outlays. In any event, between 1960 and 1962, the deficit itself—that gap between spending and earnings overseas—averaged a little less than $3 billion a year.

In an economy producing more than $500 billion a year, $3 billion is not an overwhelming amount. To be sure, the United States could not run such a deficit forever unless foreigners had an unquenchable appetite for dollars. But they haven't. The Europeans and others who have been accumulating dollars for their goods, their shares of stock and their services to American bases, want their own currency or some

---

* Foreign aid will add little to future deficits because so much of it is now tied. That means that the dollars given or loaned abroad must be spent in the United States for American goods.

† The figure is inflated somewhat because government aid programs pay for some of the exports. However, Lary estimated that this subsidy was just about equal to the nonmilitary services that Americans also provided for foreigners.

universally accepted equivalent. Partly because of tradition, partly because of convenience and partly because of an atavistic belief in a Platonically ideal currency, gold is regarded as that universal equivalent.

So the Europeans acquiring dollars from, say, Chrysler's expenditures on a French plant or the Pentagon's outlays for troops in Germany, turn in the American currency and demand American gold. While the United States' supply of gold is still the largest in the world—$16 billion at the end of 1962 —it does have a finite limit. In other words, as long as the present and curious international monetary arrangements continue, the balance of payments deficit must be halted at some point in time. And as long as no new curbs are placed on investing and military spending overseas, it must be halted by more painful measures.

Bankers and businessmen discovered the deficit as a weapon late in Eisenhower's second term and, with the enthusiastic support of many economists, have used it as a club against programs they dislike.

They argue that the deficit imposes a new discipline on the United States, that the deficit must be overcome by greater sales abroad, and that this can be accomplished only by keeping prices of American goods below those of foreigners. In its crudest version, this view implies several lines of policy, all comforting to standard business thought. Government spending (at least civilian spending) must be held down because government spending pushes up prices; labor's wage demands must be repressed because higher wages cause higher prices; interest rates must be kept up because investors will invest their funds in the United States only if they can get a bigger return than they could abroad; conversely, investors will cash in their dollar holdings if interest rates overseas are higher. In public, there was much hand-wringing over the nation's parlous state; in private, orthodox business leaders must have rejoiced over the fact that the only solutions on which sound men could agree happened to coincide with the things that sound men always wanted anyway.

President Kennedy displayed his credentials for the club of sound men in his first month in office. One of his earliest messages, on February 6, 1961, summoned Congress to enact a variety of measures designed to check the gold flow. The problem, Kennedy said, "justifies concern but not panic or alarm." The President's first Economic Report called the deficit a "critical problem" and declared that the need to increase exports "is a task of highest priority, and one which gives heightened significance to the maintenance of price stability and the rapid increase of productivity at home."

Several consequences flowed from this preoccupation with the small balance of payments deficit. First, the Administration threw its weight behind a new experiment in monetary management. The Federal Reserve was persuaded to attempt to keep up interest rates on loans of short duration while reducing rates on those of long duration. This split personality was designed to keep dollars from going overseas with the lure of high short-term rates and to encourage domestic borrowing with lower long-term rates. It is not clear whether this kept any investments from straying abroad. But the decision to prop up short-term interest rates may have choked off some borrowing at home that could have quickened the pace of recovery.

Just as important, those who urged a more ambitious federal program to spur recovery, something richer than the Eisenhower recipe, could be silenced by the grim formula: the balance of payments won't permit it. But any suggestion that the deficit could be overcome by temporarily curbing investors' appetites for foreign shares or limiting corporate outlays for new foreign plants was greeted as heresy. Oddly enough, those paragons of financial propriety, the Swiss, have restrained capital outflows when necessary for more than a generation.

In sum, the Administration's concern with the balance of payments deficit ran in the grooves marked out by the most orthodox banking thought. Ironically, at the end of the Administration's second year, European officials were telling New Frontier agents that their austerity was misplaced. The Europeans, quietly prompted by the New Frontier's more aggressive economists, were arguing that a more expansive federal program, one that would directly stimulate output, employment and growth, was much more likely to end the deficit. A lustier American economy, it was said, would yield higher profits. This would attract foreign investors and keep American funds at home; at the same time, the higher profit rates from increased production would encourage corporations to hold their prices in check. By 1963, the President had adopted this argument to bolster his case for reducing income taxes. Later in the year, he finally took the first cautious step towards inhibiting the flow of investment dollars abroad by proposing a tax on foreign securities.

Kennedy's devotion to respectable economic doctrine was underlined again in his strenuous effort to pass the celebrated trade bill. The Trade Expansion Act of 1962 was regarded by the White House as the single most important piece of legislation in its first half term. It is certainly a masterful invocation of nineteenth century liberal economic thought. But there is little in it to give sleepless nights to Adam Smith, David Ricardo, John Stuart Mill or corporations and banks with interests abroad. Described by its army of official and unofficial press agents as a "bold new program," the measure gives the President unprecedented powers to reduce duties on foreign products in return for cuts in the tariffs on American goods. It holds out the hope, in other words, of considerably freer trade, especially between the

United States and the resurgent European economies. The issue of free trade could split a nation in 1846 when English landowners savagely resisted passage of the Corn Laws. But it could hardly be called revolutionary in an advanced industrial nation a century later. So, powerful corporations who had vastly increased their stake in Europe, the leaders of the Chamber of Commerce and the AFL-CIO united to crush the parochial interests seeking protection against foreign goods. The Administration's relatively easy triumph surprised some political writers; students of the American power structure were less impressed.

While Kennedy's treatment of the Business Council, anti-recession measures, balance of payments and trade bill all comported with the standard doctrine of important segments of business, his angry quarrel with Chairman Blough of Big Steel appeared to break the pattern. Indeed, after the famous clash, some sophisticated observers spoke of a new Kennedy "opening to the left" and predicted that the President's anchor on the right, Treasury Secretary C. Douglas Dillon, would lose his role as the Cabinet's economic strong man.

Perhaps no domestic incident of the Administration's first three years has been so misunderstood. The confusion has arisen because conventional wisdom attributed political motives to the President and economic concerns to Blough; in fact, the very reverse better explains what happened.

The dramatic clash over steel prices had its roots in the Administration's wage policy, a policy designed to check pay increases. If public rhetoric is any guide, no subject is nearer to the hearts of the nation's corporation leaders and small businessmen. In season and out, they preach the virtues of abstinence from higher wages. The archetypal speech declares that most costs are ultimately wage costs, that costs determine prices. So, the argument goes, reduce wage demands and you will hold down prices, avoiding the curse of inflation, balance of payments deficits and a variety of other evils that sound men abhor. Since labor unions obstinately refuse to recognize that their members' self-interest lies in lower wages, businessmen talk wistfully of splintering union bargaining power. The speeches and pamphlets of the Chamber of Commerce and National Association of Manufacturers are filled with solutions along these lines. They reflect an almost hypnotic belief that a new application of the antitrust laws to unions, limiting the numbers for whom any union can bargain, will achieve Nirvana.

The Kennedy administration adopted some of the analysis if not the solution of this business literature. Despite high and persistent unemployment of men and resources since 1957, the new regime made stable prices one of its central concerns. And this meant, among other things, inventing some device to restrain labor's wage demands.

Kennedy, and his knowledgeable first Secretary of Labor, Arthur J. Goldberg, never seriously considered the power-reducing answer of the business literature. For one thing, union leaders comprised an important sector of the Administration's support. For another, it is questionable whether the creation of more, smaller unions would bring about the end that businessmen sought. It could lead to intensified competition among those unions with each trying to outbid the other's demands for bigger pay; industrial peace might be subjected to more frequent and intensive strains; undisciplined union leaders, with a much smaller stake in the existing state of affairs, could well be thrown up.

Most important, extending the scope of the antitrust laws would mean a radical shift in the nation's institutional structure. But plainly neither Kennedy nor his advisers had much taste for wide departures from the status quo.

The problem confronting Kennedy, then, was this: how to curb wage increases within the established union order. The answer had been perceived dimly by Eisenhower: mobilize public opinion, particularly on key wage bargains. The strategy was tried with some success in the 1959 steel negotiations. The combination of a shrinking demand for steel labor, Presidential exhortation, employer resistance and a long strike finally produced a package of pay and benefits less than half as large as the one negotiated three years earlier. But the Eisenhower approach lacked precision; it was too much of an ad hoc affair.

The new regime refined the technique in the wage and price guideposts set up in the President's first Economic Report. These guideposts established the general principle that wage increases should not exceed the gains in workers' output or productivity. This same principle had been expressed repeatedly by Eisenhower. It implies no change in the relative shares of labor and the other claimants for the economic pie. It aims at preventing any increase in the labor costs of a ton of steel, pound of rubber, one automobile and any other unit of production.

To this general principle, the Administration listed some exceptions. It described several instances in which wages should exceed or fall short of productivity gains. The Administration also urged restraint by corporations in setting prices and outlined conditions when prices should be raised or lowered.

But the thrust of the message was directed at wages. This was made clear by the statistics tacked onto the guideposts. Eisenhower's administration had been accused of vague rhetoric because it had never defined the appropriate productivity standard against which "good" and "bad" wage increases could be measured. The Kennedy economists were guilty of no such omission. Their economic report suggested several very specific standards, ranging from 2.6 percent to 3.5 percent for the whole economy.

The Economic Report did not flatly say that wage increases generally should fall within this range. But popular discussion promptly and properly assumed that the Administration ,wanted increases kept near the middle of this band or near 3 percent. It is doubtful that a single union leader is unaware of this 3 percent standard; it is equally doubtful that corporate officials, apart from the technicians in their bureaucracy, were aware that the guideposts also indicated price policy until after the blowup in steel. The wage standards were sharp enough to have an impact on collective bargaining; the price discussion was too academic and imprecise to guide any corporate price setter.

One of the leading Administration architects of the new policy declared: "Our focus is on taking the wage push out of the wage-price spiral. The range of the economy over which wage increases can spread is much wider than the rippling effect of any price increase."

Here, then, was the strategic target: limit wage increases. Kennedy, like Eisenhower, made a tactical decision to focus on steel. The reasons were simple. Steel, the President said, is a bellwether industry whose conduct has a persuasive effect on that of other industries. Blough's chairmanship of the Business Council was a chance symbol of steel's significance. Moreover, in purely economic terms, steel itself is an important industrial cost, a principal material in everything from nails to rails, from autos to skyscrapers. The central role of steel was underscored in two Congressional studies, by Gardiner Means for the Senate Antitrust and Monopoly Subcommittee and by Otto Eckstein and Gary Fromm for the Joint Economic Committee. They had shown that price increases in steel and steel-using products had accounted for the bulk of the overall price increases in the mid-1950's.

The Administration launched its campaign to hold down steel wages late in the summer of 1961. In the face of rumors that the industry was planning another price rise on October 1, the President took the extraordinary step of writing a public letter to the chiefs of the twelve leading steel companies. The key paragraph said:

> If the industry were now to forego a price increase, it would enter collective bargaining negotiations next spring with a record of three and a half years of price stability. It would clearly then be the turn of the labor representatives to limit wage demands to a level consistent with continued price stability. The moral position of the steel industry next spring —and its claim to the support of public opinion—will be strengthened by the exercise of price restraint now.

In plain English, the President was saying, "If you fellows don't raise prices, I'll help you hold the union down."

This was no empty offer. The steel union's leaders were among the President's staunchest supporters. His Labor Secretary, Goldberg, had been the chief counsel and negotiator for the union until he entered the Cabinet.

There was no price increase on October 1 and the President acted to fulfill his pledge. He and Goldberg met privately with David McDonald, the president of the United Steelworkers, and with Blough. Goldberg was in close touch with the bargaining from start to finish. It is impossible to determine how much weight this had compared to the influence of the President's public appeals, the still-shrinking demand for steel labor and the memory of the bitter four-month strike of 1959. But the outcome precisely matched the Administration's order. The union agreed on March 31 to an increase publicly estimated at 2.5 percent and privately figured at less. It was the smallest gain since the war and well down at the bottom of the guidepost range. Just as steel price policy powerfully influences the price policies of other corporations, so steel wages have a magnetic effect on demands in other industries. Goldberg, Kennedy and the President's Council of Economic Advisers were congratulating themselves on a successful wage policy.

At this crucial point, ten days after the new contract was signed, Blough told the country and the President that Big Steel was raising prices about $6.00 a ton. The President's seemingly impulsive attack on U.S. Steel is now explicable. Apart from the deliberate personal challenge to the President, Blough's action threatened to destroy the carefully constructed wage-price policy. If the increase held, unions would ignore the guideposts and bargaining would be a simple matter of extracting whatever could be gotten. Not only unions would be given a green light; plenty of corporations were waiting for steel to bell the cat and would follow steel's lead upward.

The President himself explained his conduct in just such terms during a television interview at the end of the year. He said he had acted as strongly as he did,

> . . . because there was an issue of good faith involved. The steel union had accepted the most limited settlement that they had had since the end of the second war, they had accepted it . . . in part, I think, because I said that we could not afford another inflationary spiral . . . if I had not attempted to use my influence to have the companies hold their prices stable, I think the union could have rightfully felt that they had been misled. In my opinion, it would have . . . made it impossible for us to exert any influence from the public point of view in the future on these great labor-management disputes . . .

Even Blough later acknowledged that the President's vehemence must have been inspired by the effect of the price increase on labor. The U.S. Steel Chairman said: "I believe that he (Kennedy) and Secretary Goldberg felt that an increase in steel prices, following the early wage negotiations, would be viewed as evidence that the Administration's policies were adverse to labor's interests."

In any event, Blough had demonstrated a remarkable lack of concern for his corporation's economic interest in limiting wage demands. And if Blough thought the corporation did have a greater economic interest in higher prices than in holding down wages, why did such a sophisticated executive choose such a crude way of imposing the price increase? He picked the very moment when the nation was most aware of the union's restraint. He gave the President no advance warning of Big Steel's action, but handed Kennedy a press release at the same time that the rise was announced to the public. Finally, and most importantly, Blough chose to raise prices on all products at once, across the board. Had U.S. Steel nibbled away at the lid on prices, raising one steel product here, lowering another less important one there and stretching the whole process out over several months, public opinion could not have been mobilized and Presidential wrath would probably not have been incited.

U.S. Steel's conduct leads to a belief that Blough and his hierarchs were most concerned with the guideposts' implications for corporate power. As a leader of leaders, Blough apparently wanted to discredit the guideposts and thereby smash the government's attempt to influence wages and prices. For even though the guideposts were directed chiefly at wages, their existence implied some limits on corporate freedom of action as well. They meant that the government might at some future point define with more precision appropriate pricing behavior for corporations. Finally, the construction of guideposts conflicted with another folk belief of most small businessmen and many big ones as well, the notion that government must never violate the sanctity of free markets, that wages and prices are best determined by the private actions of private men.

In a magazine article reviewing the affair eight months later, Blough solemnly concluded: "I do not think it in the public interest in peacetime for anyone, including those of Presidential rank, to substitute his own action for the action of the marketplace by trying to set prices for any competitive product."

Blough has persistently denied that his aims were ideological. He has insisted that his motives were purely commercial. However, Professor Grant McConnell of Chicago University has shed some new light on this question. He discovered that U.S. Steel's commercial department was dubious about the increase that Blough tried to bull through. In other words, the Big Steel executives best acquainted with the economic state of the steel market thought that any increase would be a business mistake.

There is a touch of irony in this affair. According to the conventional business mind, Kennedy proved once and for all his hostility to business by cracking down on Blough. In fact, it appears that Kennedy cracked down on Blough to save a policy of wage restraint that lies near to the hearts of right-thinking businessmen.

However, businessmen big and small denounced the President even if they regarded Blough as "clumsy." Corporate face had been scratched. A sudden drop in already sagging stock prices heightened the animus. At Union League Clubs, in the Dusquesne Club in Pittsburgh and in other executive fortresses, Kennedy was denounced with a fervor once reserved for Franklin Roosevelt. There was a bizarre and ugly viciousness in all this. But it had its effect. By the end of 1962, the White House was throwing out hints that selective price increases on some steel products would not be objected to. The President had displayed a cool indifference to the attempt of Senator Estes Kefauver of Tennessee to make a close and possibly embarrassing study of steel costs and profits.

The guideposts had dominated much of the economic discussion early in the year; now there were clear signs that less Presidential attention would be paid to them. In his 1963 Economic Report, Kennedy "reaffirmed" the guideposts but this was generally regarded as ritual obeisance.

Exactly 364 days after Big Steel's abortive move, the industry took the hint. A second echelon firm, Wheeling Steel Corp., acted as scout and announced a scattering of increases. Two days later, the President signaled that all was well, declaring that selective price rises "are not incompatible with a framework of general stability." The rest of the producers scrambled aboard. U.S. Steel modestly waited for others to move first but actually established the ultimate levels of increase. The over-all rise amounted to about 1 percent and Kennedy publicly hailed this as "restraint."

Again, the timing was curious. The increases were posted just before the United Steelworkers could reopen their contract on May 1 for wage negotiations. The price moves were an open invitation to the union for stiffer demands than it might otherwise have made. This probably suited the Steelworkers; it also suited other industries who had been impatiently waiting for excuses to raise prices.

This does not mean that the President could have done much more than acquiesce in the new round of markups. Even if he wanted, he could not have repeated his 1962 performance and expected it to succeed. But his failure to follow that earlier attack with proposals for some new institutional arrangements to deal with corporate pricing power is symptomatic. Immediately after the 1962 rollback, the President might have exploited his success by calling for some continuing mechanism that would insure well-defined public considerations in the decisions of private centers of economic power. One New Frontiersman, Solicitor General Archibald Cox, suggested just this. But he was pointedly ignored. Indeed,

Blough had originally increased prices to ward off such a prospect. His temporary failure alerted the rest of the business community to what was at stake and their resultant outcry led to the successful price rise of a year later. So, the Kennedy administration closed the books on the steel affair, marching in step once again with corporate leaders.

Does this summary make proper allowance for the limitations on the President's freedom of action? If there were flaws, don't they lie in the people and the setting, not the Administration? A complacent and affluent society, a conventional judgment runs, wouldn't accept the creative programs that President Kennedy really wanted.

This essay does not attempt to divine what the public will accept or to estimate the possible effect of strong leadership on the led. It more modestly attempts to put some recent history in order. However, in at least one sector of economic policy, it can be said that the President displayed considerable energy, persistence and leadership. This is the crucial area of taxes. In some ways, the Kennedy tax programs offer the best guide to his Administration's economic tastes.

2. Blue Chips and Tax Carrots

No DEPTH ANALYSIS of any government's economic psyche can be undertaken without a close scrutiny of its tax policies. Indeed, much of the world's history has turned on taxes. The very landmarks of western freedom, England's Glorious Revolution of 1688, the American and the French Revolutions all revolved to no small extent around tax disputes. The Supreme Court observed in 1819 that the power to tax involves the power to destroy but this is an incomplete statement. In the modern world, the state's tax reach is so pervasive that the power to tax is also the power to create new industries and new men of wealth. In the United States, the tax system is a crucial reference point for business decisions. Taxes play a large part in determining a firm's investment, output, pricing and inventory policy. They exert a powerful influence on the quality of the theater, the style of restaurants and the manner in which the wealthy play. Most important, the structure of taxes goes a long way in deciding who gets what and how much.

To understand the tax policies of the Kennedy administration, the tax objectives of businessmen should be kept in mind. In general, they aim at two parallel targets. Like everyone else, businessmen don't like paying taxes and seek ways to shift the burden to other groups. Secondly, businessmen generally pursue an ideological goal. They want to reduce the government's role in economic life (apart from weapons or federal purchases from and subsidies to their own firms) by shrinking government revenues. In pursuit of both ends, business organizations have sought three principal changes. The direction of these changes doesn't vary although the details do. Before Kennedy's program had taken shape and encouraged businessmen to raise their sights, their tax objectives in the three most sensitive areas followed the patterns outlined below.

· A broad cut in the personal income tax rates with the deepest reductions in the highest income brackets. Thus, in a visionary scheme promoted by the National Association of Manufacturers, the top bracket rate would drop from 91 percent to 42 percent, the bottom bracket rate from 20 percent to 15 percent and brackets in between would be squeezed more or less in proportion. In other words, the tax theoretically imposed on income over $200,000 would be slashed more than 50 percent; the tax on incomes under $2000 would be lowered only one-quarter. This would not only reduce the total take, but it would compel the bottom income groups to carry relatively more of the tax load.

· A deep slice in the corporate income tax. This had been standing at 52 percent on profits above $25,000. In a model constructed by the Committee for Economic Development, an organ of corporate powers, this rate would ultimately sink to 42 percent.

· A further slash in corporate levies by reducing the income subjected to taxes. This would be accomplished by increasing the deduction or depreciation allowance for investment in machinery, factories and similar items. A homely example shows how this works. A representative firm, Deductalot Inc., wants the rules of the tax game changed so that it can subtract from its total or gross income a larger amount for the wear and tear or depreciation of its machinery. The bigger the amount that Deductalot can subtract, the smaller will be the net income on which it is taxed and the smaller will be its payment to the federal government. Deductalot and business generally want this depreciation allowance changed in two ways. They want to subtract from their taxable income an especially large amount in the first year they purchase a machine. They also want to subtract bigger amounts than they have been permitted in each succeeding year of the machine's life.*

These three proposals have a common ground. They would lower all taxes for the well-to-do and the businesses they own and manage. However, broad public support can't be won with arguments of naked selfish interest. So businessmen have invented an elaborate welfare rationale to justify their position. In simple form, the argument goes like this: enlarged investment in new products and expanding industries is the engine to drive the economy onward and upward. The more investment is stimulated, the more investment will increase and the faster will be the nation's gain in output of goods and service. More savings are required to finance this enlarged investment. The poor can't save but the rich can. So, cut the taxes of the rich the most because they are the chief source of savings. Similarly, reduce corporation income taxes and corporations will have more funds to invest. Finally, give investment itself a direct stimulus by making purchases of ma-

---

* The arithmetic can be simplified as follows: Assume Deductalot sells $1 million worth of widgets, has expenses of $400,000 and is allowed to subtract $100,000 for depreciation. Its tax bill would be 52 percent of $500,000 (1 million minus 500,000) or $260,000. If the rules are changed so that Deductalot can subtract $200,000 for depreciation, its tax bill will be 52 percent of $400,000 (1 million minus 600,000) or $208,000. In other words, the company will save $52,000 for each additional $100,000 of depreciation allowance. If the corporate rate is dropped to 47 percent, the saving is $47,000 for each extra $100,000 of depreciation allowance.

chinery less expensive. This last is achieved by increasing those deductions for investment, by expanding depreciation allowances.

This model is not without critics. Organized labor and some economists contend that tax cuts should go chiefly to those at the bottom. Like their opposite numbers in the corporations, the labor leaders have also invented a public welfare argument. It runs in these grooves: perhaps investment is the key to faster economic growth, but justice dictates that those who have the smallest income should be first in line for tax relief. Anyway, the business program won't achieve the very goal it seeks. Investment isn't made primarily for tax reasons: Deductalot buys a new machine to increase its output mostly because it thinks it will have a larger market in which to sell. The best way to increase Deductalot's market is by bolstering aggregate demand, the purchasing power of all the people. Then Deductalot will have a stronger incentive to invest. As for savings, most business investment nowadays is paid out of the cash that corporations earn; very little is financed by tapping the tills of the wealthy through stock and bond issues. In fact, many corporations are loaded with cash, more than they know what to do with. They won't invest it until they can see those bigger markets.

The first tax plan announced by Kennedy in April 1961 focused on investment. The Administration had accepted the thesis that a direct stimulus would enlarge spending for machinery and this in turn would accelerate the pace of economic growth. Changes in tax rates were postponed, as it turned out, for nearly two years.

Thus, from the business community's standpoint, the initial Administration proposal was only half a loaf and a pretty moldy one at that. The plan did not call for the simple increase in depreciation allowances that business wanted. Instead, the Treasury concocted a new sliding scale investment credit that would give the greatest rewards to firms that bought more than their usual amounts of machinery and equipment. Conversely, the less new investment a firm made, the less it could save in taxes. This was a remarkably concentrated bit of yeast.

But if businessmen regarded this as moldy, the Administration had prepared an even less appetizing spread to cover it. The President also proposed closing several tax loopholes or privileges. Their disappearance would increase taxes from corporations and the well-to-do.

Four especially painful reforms were suggested:

1) A crackdown on expense accounts. Under the new rules firms could no longer deduct from their taxable income the costs of yachts and hunting lodges, country club memberships, entertainment at night clubs and ball games, and all the other amenities of the higher corporate life nominally designed to promote goodwill among customers. The President said, "The slogan—it's deductible—should pass from our scene."

2) A cure for tax evasion by stockholders and dividend recipients. The Treasury estimated that in 1959, for example, stockholders and depositors had simply failed to report $3.8 billion of the dividends and interest they had received. As a result they escaped $864 million in taxes. Although a popular belief holds that this is an escape hatch largely used by the poor and ignorant, the government calculated that 71 percent of the unreported dividends had gone to those with incomes of $10,000 or more. To remedy this, the Administration proposed that corporations and banks deduct 20 percent of the dividends and interest they pay out. The money withheld would be turned over to the Treasury and credited against the taxes due from the stockowners and depositors. That would put them on the same footing as wage earners whose

pay checks are automatically docked each week by their employers for federal taxes.

3) A blow at the protected tax position of international firms. International Widgets of New York can postpone paying taxes on the earnings of its subsidiary in Zurich until the Swiss offspring sends its profits back to the American parent. This encourages firms to invest overseas and to pile up untaxed earnings abroad. Apart from considerations of fair play, this promotes a bigger deficit in the balance of payments. So, the Treasury proposed compelling corporations with subsidiaries in wealthy countries to pay taxes on their subsidiaries' profits as soon as they were earned.

4) An end to the tax privileges awarded income from dividends. Thanks to an Eisenhower tax change, stockholders can subtract from their tax bill $400 for every $10,000 in dividends they receive. They can also deduct from their taxable income the first $50 of these dividends. No such gentle treatment is available, of course, for income from wages. The Treasury asked for the repeal of this 4 percent tax credit and the $50 exclusion.

The business community had not bargained for anything like this and its lobbyists quickly went into action. Unlike most important Kennedy moves in the economic area, the first tax proposal reflected a remarkable degree of independence from corporate thinking.

But when the dust settled eighteen months later, the President had approved a potpourri of tax changes that resembled his original plan about as much as canned fish chowder tastes like Voisin's bouillabaise (which is still tax-deductible for businessmen). Moreover, the President had thrown in still another bone for industry. With a simple administrative order, he permitted businessmen to deduct larger amounts for the wear and tear on their machinery. This item alone will save corporations an estimated $1.5 billion annually in taxes. Ironically, the Eisenhower Treasury had also explored the possibilities of such a move. But its experts had concluded that it couldn't be done on a significant scale without express Congressional permission.

As for the bill itself, the sliding scale investment credit, delicately attuned to encourage extra investment, had disappeared. In its place was a simple tax credit for any new investment, regardless of whether it was more or less than the firm had been customarily spending. Moreover, Congress put in one extra touch. It had the effect of converting the crude investment credit into a close cousin of the jumbo first year depreciation allowance that Deductalot had hungered for all the time. (The fact that some business organizations continued to grumble even over the emasculated investment stimulus is an index of the cultural lag among executives. At any rate, once their accountants showed them how much the provision would save, the businessmen stopped complaining.)

There was new language about expense accounts, but the hunting lodges and night club parties had been saved. Now, in order to subtract the cost of the company yacht from the corporation's taxable income, Deductalot must claim that its officers spend more than half their cruising time on business affairs. And the government will continue to share the cost of entertaining clients at the Copacabana or a Las Vegas night club as long as the party precedes or follows a business discussion.*

Although the changes were marginal, there is a belief among

---

* In writing the legislative history of this tortured provision, Senator Jacob Javits of New York asked on the Senate floor:

"Men might take a three-hour or four-hour automobile ride or train ride before they reached the situs of entertainment?"

Senator Robert Kerr of Oklahoma, the manager of the bill, replied:
"Yes."

businessmen that expense accounts are sacred, that deductibility is a God-given right of American enterprise. So, the Commissioner of Internal Revenue was compelled to make clear in words of one syllable that nothing important had been changed. In a simple question and answer guide to the new law, the Commissioner explained that deductions are still in order among other things for entertaining businessmen's wives. It is true, the Commissioner acknowledged, that Congress has now forbidden "lavish or extravagant entertainment." But he assured everybody that he would not try to define in dollar terms how much is lavish.

Senator Albert Gore of Tennessee, a perennially disappointed tax reformer, concluded that the new expense account provision did not open the loophole any wider. But, he added, it "would make the situation worse than present law because it would give legislative endorsement to and would constitute legislative endorsement of widespread abuse, the scandalous avoidance of taxes."

Withholding remains the exclusive stigma of the wage earner. There will be no withholding of dividends and interest to prevent evasion. Instead, banks now report to the Treasury the names of interest recipients and the amounts they get. How effective this will be might be judged from the fact that a similar provision requiring reporting of dividends has been in force since 1923. But thirty-six years later, stockholders were still failing to disclose nearly one billion dollars of their dividends.

The new law ignored the problem of deferred earnings from overseas subsidiaries. It did tighten up on evasion of taxes by corporations that create paper companies in Trinidad, Panama and other tax havens. However, Dillon himself was quoted as saying that failure to deal with deferred earnings "would be but 'piddling' with the problem."

The privileged tax status of dividend income, the 4 percent credit and $50 exclusion also emerged intact. And for good measure, Congress wrote a brand new loophole into the law, one allowing corporations to deduct from their income their expenses for lobbying.

In sum, the law barely touched some important loopholes for the corporations and the wealthy which Kennedy had said he wanted to plug. On the other hand, the drastically revised investment stimulus and the increase in depreciation allowances gave business just about what it wanted in this sector. The two changes together could reduce taxes on corporations by about $2.8 billion annually.*

But couldn't it be argued that the final form of the tax bill proved very little about the Administration's inner impulses? Wasn't the President's genuine self revealed more faithfully in the original proposal of April 1961? Wasn't he helpless against a Congress dominated by crude conservatives?

That Congress is conditioned by business-minded conservatives is a plausible proposition. But the picture of a coerced President is harder to accept. The Constitution does not leave the President without resources. He could have vetoed the bill and it would have sunk without a trace. Indeed, its many provisions upset so many different interests and its chief beneficiaries understood it so poorly that Congress would gladly have aborted the measure long before it reached the President's hands. But Kennedy's lieutenants lobbied tirelessly for its passage and Kennedy himself made it an item of high urgency.

There is no reason to question the President's sincerity. He no doubt favored most of the reforms he asked for in April 1961. But the bill's ultimate shape offered a revealing glimpse of the President's preferences, of his order of priorities. In his first Economic Report, he explicitly urged "the earliest possi-

---

* In the first year they were in force, the two new rules saved business an estimated 2¼ billion dollars.

ble enactment" of the measure which was then before the House Ways and Means Committee. He declared that "the centerpiece of these proposals" is the investment credit, even stripped of its sliding scale.

Just before the Senate voted on an even looser version, Senator Joseph Clark of Pennsylvania declared that the bill could be called a "tax dodger's delight."

Clark said, "It is very difficult for me to understand why the Administration and the Treasury are willing to take a bill which is so far removed from what the President wanted."

But the Majority Leader, Senator Mike Mansfield of Montana, pulled out a letter from Dillon that undercut Clark's assumption about the President's desires. The letter said:

"The bill . . . represents a major advance toward our national goal of a revised and modernized tax system. In its tax reform provisions, the bill makes substantial headway in eliminating many long recognized abuses. The investment credit provides a significant stimulus both to economic growth and America's competitive position in the world . . . The bill . . . is a significant first step toward the reform of our present outmoded tax laws . . . I urge its . . . passage."

At least one of the President's liberal supporters cast a wistful look backward at the missing withholding provision. Senator John Carroll of Colorado remarked, "I wonder that the Administration did not give this proposal greater support. Why have we not heard more from the President?"

Senator Paul Douglas of Illinois replied, "The President made a statement last week."

"I know," said Carroll, "and I am for it. But there was no great effort made at the grassroots level."

If Kennedy was disappointed with what Congress gave him, he concealed it successfully. In signing the bill into law he said:

"This is an important bill—one possessing many desirable

features which will stimulate the economy and provide a greater measure of fairness in our tax system."

The measure, he insisted, "provides a favorable context for tax reforms to be submitted in 1963."

The new depreciation allowances and the Revenue Act of 1962 embodied only one-third of the business tax program. What about the other two-thirds, the reduction in corporate and personal income tax rates?

When the stock market stumbled for the second Blue Monday in succession on June 4, 1962, Secretary Dillon hurried to the rescue with a speech in New York that night. He promised that the Administration would seek cuts in every tax bracket to become effective the next year. The President honored Dillon's pledge and made reduction of tax rates his chief legislative goal for 1963. However, his proposals were such a mixed bag of rate cuts and "structural reforms," that they were first greeted with considerable confusion and suspicion. But after the President made clear what he really wanted, everything fell into place. The heart of the plan was the cut in rates—not reforms—and the suggested rates paralleled to a remarkable extent those urged by the United States Chamber of Commerce.

The President proposed cutting the rate in the top income bracket from 91 percent to 65 percent. At the bottom, he suggested that Congress replace the 20 percent rate with 14 percent on the first $1000 of taxable income and 16 percent on the next. The Chamber had urged the very same cut at the top; it would be less generous to the bottom, however, lowering only the take from the initial $1000 and setting that rate at 15 percent.

Going up the income scale, the Chamber proposed somewhat smaller reductions than the President. But at the $38,000 bracket and higher, the two plans were identical.

Similarly in the corporate sphere, Kennedy and the Chamber were at one. Both urged dropping the corporate income tax from 52 percent to 47 percent.

The President's reform proposals, however, were not at all to the taste of the Chamber or businessmen generally. These changes threatened to narrow or close some of the loopholes left open the year before, including the privileged tax status of dividends, estates of the wealthy and income from oil wells. The business community again filled the land with cries over these new burdens. The noise was so deafening that it threatened to drown out the essential truth, that business wanted those lower taxes at the top and the reduced rate for corporations. So the President went before a symposium of bankers to clear the air. In the course of a reply to a single question, Kennedy five times said that reforms should not get in the way of tax cuts, that rate reduction came first and reforms a distant second. The message was unmistakable. An elite body of corporation leaders promptly responded to the Treasury's appeal for aid and set about convincing Congress and the nation that businessmen really did want lower taxes. After his first meeting with these crusaders for the obvious, the President underscored his point again. He said that the business hierarchs' support for tax cuts "is far more significant" than their dislike of the reforms. Among those enlisted in the crusade were Roger Blough; Frederick R. Kappel, chairman of American Telephone & Telegraph Co. and the new chairman of the Business Council; David Rockefeller, president of the Chase Manhattan Bank; and Frederic G. Donner, chairman of General Motors Corp. In fact, many of the committee were also members of the Business Council that had once troubled Secretary Hodges.

There was every reason for them to climb aboard. The simple fact is that the Kennedy proposals offered gains of substance to those in the upper brackets. Consider the cuts in personal rates alone. Some 2.4 percent of all taxpayers, those with taxable incomes of $20,000 or more, stood to pick up $2.3 billion. But the 39.6 percent with taxable incomes of $5000 or less would gain only $1.5 billion. Looking at a more extreme case, the 200,000 wealthiest taxpayers would get an average cut of $4600 and the lowest 20 million about $75 each.

George T. Altman, a tax lawyer writing in *The Nation,* calculated how the Kennedy-proposed tax rates would affect selected persons up and down the income scale. For example, he figured that a married couple with two children that had been taking home $4580 could look forward to a gain of $124 or 2.7 percent. Conversely, a family with $143,454 left after the existing taxes would gain $238,996 or 166.5 percent. To be sure, all these disparities would be narrowed by passage of the Kennedy reforms. But the President himself had made clear that he would be well satisfied with limited change in this area. Indeed, the Administration embraced another version of the bill in the summer of 1963 that abandoned most of the reforms and provided even greater maldistribution of rewards.

In any case, preoccupation with the President's proposals for personal income taxes obscures the effect of his suggestions for additional relief to corporations. They stood to gain $2.6 billion a year from the rate cuts. And this would come on top of the tax savings they had received in 1962, $1.5 billion from the new depreciation allowances and $1.3 billion from the new investment credit. Some portion of all this extra cash flow would swell dividends; another portion enhanced the value of corporation shares. Since stock ownership is heavily concentrated in the upper brackets,* the wealthiest were in line for even more help.

* Share holdings are distributed much less broadly than labels like "People's Capitalism" suggest. The University of Michigan Survey Research Center has estimated that only a sixth of the nation's families owned a single share in 1960. Within that narrow group, nearly two-thirds of the value of all shares

It is not surprising that the Treasury was able to win the distinguished business leaders to its cause.

The similarity between the Kennedy tax policies and the Chamber's program did not mean that the President was insensitive to the public welfare. The notion that everything business supports is suspect is a conditioned reflex, not an exercise in analysis. At this point, only one question has been raised: to what extent did Kennedy's economics harmonize with those of the corporate world?

Public attention (and ours, so far) centered on the contents of the Kennedy tax programs. But this ignores a crucial implication of the very decision to cut taxes in 1963. Taxes were to be cut to stimulate a lackluster economy. However, the President might have chosen instead to rely primarily on a sharp increase in federal spending. His choice of tax reduction was a triumph of no small proportions for business thinking.

Why was a stimulant needed? From the time the Administration took office, it had fretted over the economy's recent and peculiar performance. Since 1957, the country had gone through two recessions and two unsatisfactory recoveries. From 1957 through 1962, more than 5 percent of the work force had continuously been unable to find jobs. All during this period, the economy's growth barely kept ahead of the rise in population, averaging only 1.2 percent a year. A broad spectrum of economists believed that the chief cause for this unhappy state of affairs was the restraining hand of the federal budget. The tax structure was designed to repress wartime inflation. That era has ended but its revenue-raising heritage remains. While federal expenditures have been rising, they haven't accelerated fast enough to overcome the tax brake.

---

were held by families in the top 14 percent of the income band. In another study, Robert J. Lampman of Wisconsin calculated that the richest one percent of all adults owned three-quarters of all the stock in 1953.

This does not mean that government spending did not rise under Kennedy. It did, and a bit faster than under Eisenhower. In Eisenhower's last three fiscal years, federal cash payments to the public rose $16.1 billion or nearly 20 percent. In Kennedy's three fiscal years, they were scheduled to rise $23 billion or nearly 25 percent. However, the difference was more than accounted for by enlarged defense and space expenditures, those government outlays to which few businessmen object.

The added military expenditures might be viewed as the Administration's unacknowledged stimulant for the economy. Its publicly proclaimed remedy, however, was the 1963 tax program.

The problem has two separate but related sides. At any given point in time, the government was draining too much in taxes from the spending stream and failing to make good this deficit with enough spending of its own. The "deficit" referred to here is not some abstract accounting figure of government debt but the more important deficit of inadequate demand. Here common logic and economics are at one. The more the federal government takes, the less there is left for individuals and business firms to spend. The less total spending there is, the smaller are the markets for the products of business and the less demand there is for workers. This holds true as long as the government fails to make up for the short-fall in demand by enlarging its own spending for the products of industry and the services of labor.

The other side of the problem is tied to the collection of taxes during recoveries. As the economy moves from slump to boom, incomes of individuals and of business firms rise. But the government's tax take rises even faster. Again, unless the government accelerates its spending at the same pace, the tax withdrawals put a brake on demand. As a result, the economy tends to flatten out and then fall back, the production of goods and services increases at slower and slower rates until it actually declines, employment doesn't keep pace with the rise in population and the increased efficiency of workers. In brief, the recoveries are aborted and large numbers of men and plants are left idle.

(The very opposite process then takes place. In a slump, the government's tax collections fall much faster than the decline in incomes and output. As long as government spending isn't cut as rapidly as the drop in tax collections, the government is strengthening total demand. This brings the slump in incomes and output to a halt and the economy reverses itself again. It is this automatic stabilizing feature of the tax structure that brought the 1958 and 1960 recessions to an end before the Eisenhower and Kennedy anti-recession programs took hold. In other words, the tax-spending brake not only arrests recoveries; it also halts slumps.)

Either one of two solutions will solve this problem: release the tax brake by cutting the rates or increase the total demand by stepping up federal expenditures.

One school, popularly identified with Professor John Kenneth Galbraith, would pump up demand by expanding federal expenditures. This group argues that the nation's most urgent tasks are in the undernourished public sector—building schools, clearing slums, enlarging recreation facilities, attacking traffic jams, wiping out city smog and directly assaulting poverty. Tax cuts that largely feed private affluence should wait until these demands are satisfied.

Businessmen, of course, generally regard this kind of thinking as a disguised form of socialism. They deny that the public sector is starved; or if it is, they say local government should somehow sustain it. In any event, the federal government is Too Big and these schemes would make it bigger. Thus, the only acceptable solution—again apart from military spending—is to cut taxes.

Some businessmen believe they see another virtue in cutting taxes. They think that lower revenues will force the government to reduce its spending and thereby diminish its role. If this happened, of course, it would defeat the objective of filling the depleted income or demand stream. But material interests often yield to ideological concerns in the corporate world.

The Administration officially adopted the theory of the braking budget in its first Economic Report in January 1962. The decision to cut taxes as the brake-releasing device was announced in June. Once again, in a key area, Kennedy's economics and the business vision were at one.

                              *   *   *

Of all the myths in current political and economic literature, one of the most imaginative and furthest removed from reality portrayed President Kennedy as anti-business. In fact, in every significant area—wage policy, tax policy, international trade and finance, federal spending—the President showed a keen understanding and ready response to the essential corporate program. It is doubtful that a Republican president, historically vulnerable to the charge of "business tool," could have done as much. Indeed, Eisenhower didn't.

To be sure, most business executives will neither recognize nor acknowledge how much of their program the President attempted to execute. There are good reasons for this.

Some businessmen believe the myths cultivated by the image-makers of both major parties, that Democratic administrations are kind to labor and hard on business, that Democrats are spendthrift welfare-state proponents taking the nation down the road to socialism. Others, loyal Republicans, see through the slogans but are unwilling to endorse the other party's man. More sophisticated business leaders, equally at home in both parties, were not likely to acknowledge the support Kennedy gave business for broader tactical reasons.

They learned that the President tried to relieve rather than resist pressure; the less support they admitted they were getting, the more he was likely to give. A second and related reason has to do with business sensitivity about its own power. To proclaim the triumph of business doctrine on the New Frontier might invite retaliation and counterpressure by organized labor, farmers and other interest groups. Overt display of power in the corporate world is not only vulgar, it is unprofitable. Finally, most businessmen cling to a nostalgic vision of an earlier age, when government was smaller and life appeared to be simpler. In this view, government is best when it is felt least and sound men of affairs are in the saddle.

Even so, there was a marked shift in the business attitude towards Kennedy after his tax policies and the other main lines of the New Frontier's economics became clear. The almost hysterical cries raised after the rollback of steel prices were muted. The business community was not openly embracing Kennedy as one of its own, but a more objective tone was being heard in businessmen's public and private talk.

Charls Walker, spokesman for the nation's commercial banks, Executive Vice President of the American Bankers Association and a former aide to a Republican Treasury Secretary, said:

"Rather than being anti-business, this Administration, except for its actions during the steel price incident, has exhibited a sympathetic and constructive attitude towards the business and financial community."

In private, Roger Blough was telling questioners that the President's approach on taxes and other matters "showed a greater understanding of our industry's problems."

After the President's tragic murder, some of his aides suggested that he had planned a shift in emphasis for 1964. If the President had lived, it was said, he would have been less solicitous of business and more concerned with the welfare measures that corporate leaders generally dislike. But whatever stance the President might have adopted, the substance of his three years in office was clear to behold. It was in large measure a triumph for the corporate perspective.

President Kennedy himself was impatient with labels like "pro-business" or "anti-business" and there is much to be said for his view. In his celebrated speech at Yale University on economic myths, he declared that a modern economy's problems—jobs, technology and productivity—are technical, not ideological. They are not solved, he said, by "the reassuring repetition of stale phrases" mouthed by interest groups, but by engaging in "an essential confrontation with reality."

The President continued: "What is at stake in our economic decisions today is not some grand warfare of rival ideologies which will sweep the country with passion but the practical management of a modern economy. What we need is not labels and clichés but more basic discussion of the sophisticated and technical questions involved in keeping a great economic machinery moving ahead."

The President and those around him liked to be regarded as pragmatists, in the great tradition of William James. James has taught that the "only test of probable truth is what works best."

At Yale, Kennedy implied that this was his test too. Which brings us to the heart of this inquiry. Could the business-oriented policies of the New Frontier master the problems confronting the economy? Will the corporate vision bring about full employment of men and resources, quicken the sluggish pace of economic growth and bring material abundance to the surprisingly large group outside the affluent society? Is the existing economic structure capable of solving these problems, as the President implied, or are some institutional changes necessary?

3. The Visible Hands

To ANSWER these questions, President Kennedy suggested that reality must be confronted. But in economic affairs, the real and the spurious are often buried under layers of conventional belief and self-serving myth. Perhaps the most common distortion is embodied in the following contemporary fable:

"It is well to remind ourselves from time to time of the benefits we derive from the maintenance of a free market system. The system rests on freedom of consumer choice, the profit motive and vigorous competition for the buyer's dollar. By relying on these spontaneous economic forces, we secure these benefits."

The benefits are then described as the automatic production of the goods consumers want in the quantities they want them; automatic minimizing of waste in a world in which the most efficient producers triumph; encouragement of innovation and technological change through high rewards and competitive adaption.

"The free market is a decentralized regulator of our economic system. The free market is not only a more efficient decision maker than even the wisest central planning body, but even more important, the free market keeps economic power widely dispersed."

This is a contemporary restatement of Adam Smith's invisible hand. It was proclaimed by President Kennedy only a few months after he decried economic myths at Yale. The President's narrative had only marginal relevance to the modern world. Indeed, the Kennedy administration itself designed policies on a very different set of assumptions. In an atomistic, self-regulating economy there would be no point in trying techniques to restrain wage and price increases, devising tax programs to stimulate investment and worrying about the federal budget's impact on employment and output. In a world of pure and free competition, these problems solve themselves.

But the central fact about the American economy is that it is concentrated. In nearly every important manufacturing industry, a handful of firms produce a major share of the output, employ a significant portion of the work force and make the decisive investment decisions. The auto industry is dominated by a single firm with two lesser giants following behind it; in steel, three large companies control more than half of the total capacity while nine other firms own most of what is left; in electrical machinery, two great complexes stand out. While this concentration is especially visible in manufacturing, the most volatile sector of the economy, other areas like retailing and finance are shaped to some degree by a handful of leading concerns.

This overriding fact of concentration is taken for granted by the casual observer of the business scene. It is acknowledged but often ignored by economists. It is taken into account by government policy makers with reluctance and only when it intrudes on their vision with a prominence that can't be denied.

Instead of reckoning with large and concrete corporations, economists and government officials prefer to shape policy around large and impersonal abstractions. They think in terms of total demand, total employment; they manipulate broad-gauged tools like taxes, spending and the supply of money and credit. These concepts and tools were fitted together in the brilliant construction of John Maynard Keynes. His insights were apparently confirmed in World War II when the military economy's insatiable appetite for goods ended the great depression. As a result, attention has been diverted from the structure of the economy to more sweeping categories. Policy makers have examined the economy with a telescope, not a microscope. In the jargon of the professionals, the focus has been macroeconomic, not microeconomic. Only in the last few years has there been a growing, if limited, rediscovery of industry's shape. Preoccupation with the forest had hidden some important trees. Recent experience indicates that giant corporations, sometimes with the tacit support of large unions, can frustrate and upset broad-ranging policy designs.

The crucial fact of concentration has been snubbed for several reasons. This is, after all, a sensitive subject because it involves power. For a policy maker to cope with concentration can mean conflict with the strongest institutions in America.

Then, too, economists have invested considerable intellectual capital in exploring a model world of small, competing firms. If adequate account was taken of the fact that industries are generally organized by a few competitors, much of this capital stock would become obsolete.

Moreover, the existence of private power centers disturbs the soothing national belief in a pluralistic society. It is more agreeable to picture a world in which power is diffused, where one–man, one–vote expresses more than a formal political arrangement and reflects an underlying reality. Most of all, it is upsetting to acknowledge the existence of private power without public accountability. But the fact of concentration lends color to the unpleasant suggestion of Walter Adams and Horace M. Gray that America is moving towards "an Orwellian technocracy functioning under the aegis of socially irresponsible private power."

The features of the contemporary economic landscape can best be seen by comparing them with the economy of the less complicated texts, the classical world associated with Adam Smith, the simple world described by Kennedy in his account of the free market. In this setting, economic power is diffused. In every industry, no single firm is large enough to materially affect the price or supply of that industry's product. Each producer is confronted with an impersonal price, one he bears no share in making because it is determined by larger forces of supply and demand. Each producer tries to set his output so that the cost of turning out one more unit just matches this market price. In a world without price supports, this would be the situation of the wheat grower; his price would be set by forces over which he had no control.

In the classical economy of perfectly competitive industries, each producer tries to make the most profit possible. All are under continual pressure to search for cheaper methods of production and adopt the improved techniques of their peers. Happily for society, the self-interest of each producer in garnering the greatest profit insures an ideal arrangement for all. In this Smithian world, scarce resources of men, materials and investment are most efficiently distributed. Thanks to the carrot of demand and the stick of competition, resources are allocated in accord with the tastes of consumers and combined in the least wasteful fashion. The impersonal markets transmit the code for these ideal outputs through the signals of competitive prices. Thus, the invisible hand of competition rules economic activity and brings about the best of all possible material worlds.

In the everyday world, however, no such elegant mechanism is at work. Broad stretches of the economy are marked by much more personal markets in which giant firms have considerable discretion over their prices and a great deal more. General Motors is simply not in the same position as the wheat producer whose personal decision to raise or lower his price, increase or cut back his acreage makes no difference to the price of wheat generally or the amount of wheat that will be sold.

On Capitol Hill, in the inspirational literature emitted by business and in the cruder textbooks, the small producer is hero. Indeed, if sheer numbers counted, he ought to be. Like the poor who must be blessed because there are so many of them, small firms make up the bulk of the business population. In 1962, there were about four and three-quarter million companies in the United States and the vast majority were small by any definition. However, their number is a poor index to the importance of small business in the economy. In a study covering data through 1958, Norman R. Collins and Lee E. Preston found that the 100 largest industrial corporations owned 30 percent of the assets of all manufacturing, mining and distribution companies. Even this aggregation of giants has its leaders. The 20 largest owned more than half of the group's assets and the four biggest, more than a fifth.

The Census Bureau periodically computes the degree of concentration for individual industries. The last survey also in 1958 disclosed that four* or fewer manufacturers account for more than half of their industry's sales in many sectors of the economy.

Here is the share taken by the top four in some leading industries, all with sales over $1 billion:

* The government does not break down its estimates and specify the shares of the biggest firm or top two or three in an industry. The calculations are limited to groupings of four on the somewhat dubious ground that a more refined count would give competitors information they now lack. Thus General Motor's 50 percent share of the auto market is supposedly a secret to be kept from Ford and Chrysler.

Motor vehicles and parts . . . . 75 percent
Steelworks and rolling mills . . . . 53 percent
Aircraft . . . . 59 percent
Aircraft engines . . . . 56 percent
Organic chemicals . . . . 55 percent
Tires and inner tubes . . . . 74 percent
Cigarettes . . . . 79 percent
Tin cans and other tinware . . . . 80 percent
Synthetic fibers . . . . 78 percent
Tractors . . . . 69 percent

After an earlier 1954 survey appeared, Carl Kaysen and Donald F. Turner summarized these little noticed Census tables. In manufacturing, they listed 147 industries that sold their products across the country. Of these 147 industries, they distinguished 58 that were highly concentrated and another 46 that were simply concentrated.* In other words, two-thirds of the manufacturing industries with national markets are organized in a fashion that lies outside the world of classical economics. The typical manufacturing industry then is dominated by a handful of large competitors. They are not confronted by, but play a large role in determining, their prices.

Impressive as these figures may be, they only begin to reflect the extent to which the American economy rests on the giants. There are, after all, many industries; some, like rayon and cotton, compete with each other. So, to center on concentration in one industry might seem to exaggerate the lack of competition. However, another way of looking at the economy is to measure the portion of all industrial output produced by the large companies. Again, the figures don't fit the model

* A highly concentrated industry is one in which the eight largest firms account for half or more of the sales and the twenty largest, 75 percent or more. In a concentrated industry, the top eight account for at least a third of the sales and the top twenty, less than 75 percent.

of Adam Smith. For in 1958, the 50 largest corporations produced nearly one-quarter (23 percent) of all the value added in the manufacturing process. The biggest 100 firms claimed nearly a third (30 percent) and the top 200 almost two-fifths (38 percent).

Economists have been arguing for years over whether concentration is growing greater, smaller or holding steady. Are the big firms carving out an increasing portion of the economic domain? A look at individual industries is inconclusive. Since World War II, some like oil refining, aircraft engines, motors and generators and cigarettes have become less compact. The share of the four biggest companies in each has been slipping. Others, like motor vehicles and parts, bread and related products, paper and board products and ship building and repairing have become more concentrated. The big four have been gaining ground.

But a second look at the very biggest giants offers a strong hint that more and more of manufacturing is being drawn into fewer and fewer hands. Between 1947 and 1958, the top 50 firms enlarged their share of the industrial pie from 17 percent to 23 percent; the biggest 200 from 30 percent to 38 percent. In other words, the 200 greatest corporations increased their slice of a much bigger pie by more than one-quarter. The concentration of assets in the hands of the 100 industrial giants has also been growing slowly. Between 1948 and 1958, their share of all industrial assets rose from 26.7 percent to 29.8 percent. The top 20 firms were gaining on the second 80 at about the same pace.

If, however, concentration is shrinking in as many industries as it is growing, how did the largest corporations expand their sphere? The answer apparently is this: the big concerns have been breaking outside the bounds of their traditional industries and buying up firms in more or less unrelated fields. Since the end of World War II, the nation has been moving through the third great wave of corporate marriages in American economic history. Typically, these postwar mergers have united a big firm in one field with a smaller firm in another. These weddings are much more likely to escape the prohibitions of the antitrust laws than mergers between two clearly competing firms in the same industry.

The conglomerate merger, as these marriages across industry lines are called, is not a new phenomenon on the American scene. Partly as a result of mergers, General Motors has for years been a leading producer of diesel locomotives, refrigerators and trucks as well as autos. But the rapid spread of conglomerates is new and adds another dimension to the model of concentration in any one industry. Some of the corporate giants are not only powers in their native industry; they are figures of substance in several other industries as well. In the eleven years from 1950 through 1961, the 500 biggest industrial firms picked up 3404 other companies, an average of seven apiece. The top 200 acquired 1943 or an average of nearly ten each. Thus, Ford Motor Co. bought up Philco Corp., a major producer of radio and television sets. The General Dynamics Corp. embraced firms making missiles, radio and television equipment, building materials, welding apparatus and industrial gases. Textron, Inc., as its name implies, was once primarily a textiles producer; by 1961, textiles accounted for only 15 percent of its business and in 1963 it sold its last textile mill. Meanwhile Textron has taken under its wing makers of calendars, padding for auto seats, radar antennas, screw fasteners, brooms, storm doors, bathroom fixtures, plywood, watches, eyeglasses and shoes among others.

When these giants buy their way into highly competitive industries, the nature of competition within those industries changes from the classical model. The giant parent can use his greater resources to support price and output behavior by a subsidiary that the junior firm on its own could not afford. The Federal Trade Commission noted in 1948: "The giant conglomerate corporation may attain an almost impregnable economic position. Threatened with competition in any one of its various activities, it may sell below cost in that field, offsetting its losses through profits made in other lines —a practice which is frequently explained as one of meeting competition. The conglomerate corporation is thus in a position to strike out with great force against smaller business in a variety of different industries."

One further characteristic of the economic landscape should be noted: the landmarks are pretty stable. If life were perilous for the giants, if yesterday's pigmy became tomorrow's colossus, the economy would be much more competitive than concentration figures taken at one point in time suggest. But this does not happen. The behemoths generally maintain their dominance. Of the 50 largest manufacturers in 1958, some 34 were in this same sphere in 1947. The remaining 16 rose to their new eminence from the only slightly less exclusive top 200. In the postwar period, the industrial elite have not had to contend with many upstart new rich.

A relief map of the American economy, then, does not show a plateau of myriad indistinguishable, atomistic competitors. In region after region, distinct mountains emerge. Moreover, many of these mountains have foothills trailing off beyond their historic industrial boundaries. And towering above all the ranges are perhaps 200 corporate peaks whose features give the economy its essential contour.

The view of a market from a giant's executive suite is vastly different from the perspective of the Kansas wheat farmer. In the typical concentrated industry, the dominant corporations tend to abandon the law of the competitive jungle and substitute safety. Instead of survival of the fittest, the prevailing mode is live and let live. To be sure, there are exceptions, breakaways from the pack, harassing attacks and

defensive countermeasures. But in general, corporation executives yearn for stability. They don't seek the most profits
possible, the spur of perfectly competitive markets. Instead,
they seek satisfactory profits and institutional survival.

The typical manufacturing industry has a price leader and
several important followers. So, in steel, no price increase can
stick unless U.S. Steel goes along with it. In farm machinery,
International Harvester is top dog. In electrical machinery,
General Electric is the leader and Westinghouse the most
important follower. In autos, General Motors is the kingpin.
A Ford Motor Co. executive and a noted economist at that
once insisted that Ford copied a GM price increase—not a
decrease—"to meet competition." In this world, "meeting
competition" means touching hands with a neighbor, not
struggling with an enemy. Competition in the conventional
sense becomes largely a matter of advertising and salesman-
ship, of attempting to establish a unique quality for similar
or identical products. But competition in price, the key to
the classical code, is vitiated or wiped out entirely.

The price leader is generally the largest single producer of
a product. His followers respect the leadership as long as they
believe they would gain nothing by revolt. As price-following
companies have explained again and again to inquiring congressmen, there is no point in quoting a price below the
leader's. The leader would simply come down to the lower
price and all hands would be worse off.

If such leadership is to persist, there must be a tacit if not
an explicit understanding that no firm will attempt to alter
drastically its share of the market. If any firm does try to
enlarge its share by quoting lower prices, the system falls apart
and something resembling classical competition emerges. The
recognition that stability and order are proper corporate goals
is part of the language. The term "price cutter" is a pejorative
in the talk of most businessmen.

The practice of price leadership does not require an illegal conspiracy, does not demand that representatives of the Big Three or Four gather secretly in a hotel room to set prices and carve up markets. At least it doesn't require an unlawful arrangement as long as all firms are selling similar products that are manufactured again and again. The corporate leaders are tempted to break the antitrust law only when they sell custom-built products for individual buyers. In the steel industry, Bethlehem and Republic are generally willing to let U.S. Steel select the price for such standardized products as cold rolled sheets. But in the steel forgings branch of the industry, each product is usually tailor-made. There can be no standard price because each sale is unique and there can't be a stable division of the market because the market is not continuous. Executives of the big steel companies have not been charged with conspiring to fix prices on most of their products; however, officials from U.S. Steel, Bethlehem and others in the steel forgings business were indicted in 1962 for illegal price fixing and pleaded their unwillingness to contest the charges.

Similarly, GE, Westinghouse and their rivals don't need to meet illegally to set prices and determine market shares in standard products with continuous production runs like toasters or electrical equipment sold off the shelf from stock. Here, price leadership and the live-and-let-live philosophy can guarantee order. But generators, custom-built for a single customer, are another matter. If this business is to enjoy price stability and undisturbed market shares, its executives must conspire. And so the electrical machinery makers did meet to set prices and slice up markets for years in the great price conspiracy uncovered in 1959. The purpose of the illegal gatherings, as officials repeatedly testified, was to bring order out of chaos, to stabilize prices and apportion the business.

The price leader in a concentrated industry does not have the wide-ranging power, the discretion of a monopolist. He

has far more control over his price and his output than the
lone farmer, but there are limits to his economic power. He
must take into account the moves of his principal followers.
This was dramatically illustrated in the 1962 steel crisis.
Bethlehem, apparently frightened of retaliation by the Kennedy administration, broke away from U.S. Steel and the
other major producers to cancel its price increase. Big Steel,
in turn, was then forced to back down.*

Apart from the other members of the peer group, the price
leader is restrained by several other forces. If he sets too high
a price and earns too big a profit, he may attract new competing firms into the industry. This magnet may be more chimeri-
cal than real in some industries when the capital investment
required to operate one plant is very great. Organizing an auto
company from scratch takes enormous capital as even the
wealthy Kaiser enterprises found out when their auto baby
died in infancy after the second world war. But despite the
great capital demands in most manufacturing industries, the
danger of luring new firms is a limiting factor.

Another curb is the appetite of rival industries. Steel, for
example, must keep a wary eye on plastics, cement, aluminum
and other products which can be substituted for it if steel
prices climb too far. The government may be a limiting force
too. An excessive price or unusual profit gained through the
exercise of economic power could invite political outcry,
antitrust action, congressional investigation and other unpleasant consequences.

Finally, foreign producers constitute a limiting force. As
trade barriers go down, imports from the revived European

---

* Popular belief holds that the refusal of some smaller firms to go along
with the increase—notably Inland Steel, Kaiser Steel and Armco Steel—
was decisive in rolling it back. The evidence is far from conclusive, but it is
not likely that these junior companies could have turned the tide. They
lacked the steelmaking capacity to expand their output enough to make a
consequential dent in the business of the larger firms. However, their stand
undoubtedly embarrassed the giants who had raised prices and put added
political pressure on Bethlehem.

and Japanese industries shrink the market power of the concentrated industries. In time, steel, auto and other producers may attempt to achieve the live-and-let-live arrangements with foreign firms that have long marked the international oil business. But so far as is known, this degree of security has not yet been reached generally.

The price leader, then, is far from a free agent. But it is neither accurate nor practical to view him and his peers in the same light as the competitors of Adam Smith's world. Instead of being faced with an impersonally determined price, the industrial leader has a wide area of discretion. How this discretion is exercised, how prices are set in the modern world, has been explored by three scholars in a study for the Brookings Institution. One, Robert Lanzillotti, summarized the findings.

He reported that the typical industrial leader prices to achieve a target rate of return. The giant estimates its standard volume or "normal" output and sets prices to gain a predetermined rate of profit on this volume of sales. The profit goal is calculated as a percentage of the company's investment. If the economy is booming and the giant can sell more than its normal volume, it will take in higher profits than the target; if business slumps, the firm will probably not lower its price but simply pocket a smaller return. Over the course of any business cycle, however, the giant expects to turn out this standard volume and earn the target profit rate. Its expectations will be realized if it has selected realistic levels.

Lanzillotti has compared the target rate and actual performance for several price leaders over the 1947–1955 period. His findings are shown in the table on page 56.

Apart from General Motors, which topped its target handsomely, the price leaders came very close to their goals. More efficient followers in each industry did better; less efficient followers, not as well.

The live-and-let-live characteristics of big industry also

PRICE LEADER	TARGET RATE AFTER TAXES	YEARLY AVERAGE OF ACTUAL EARN- INGS AFTER TAXES AS A PERCENTAGE OF INVESTMENT	RANGE
General Motors	20%	26%	19.9–37%
Du Pont	*	25.9%	19.6–34.1%
General Electric	20%	21.4%	18.4–26.6%
Union Carbide	18%	19.2%	13.5–24.3%
Standard Oil (N.J.)	*	16.0%	12.0–18.9%
Johns-Manville	15%	14.9%	10.7–19.6%
Alcoa	10%	13.8%	7.8–18.7%
International Harvester	10%	8.9%	4.9–11.9%
U.S. Steel	8%†	10.3%	7.6–14.8%

* Neither Du Pont nor Standard Oil (N.J.) would give Lanzillotti a specific target rate although they said they priced with a target in mind.

† U.S. Steel apparently raised its target in the middle 1950's and this was a major force behind its successive price increases.

turn up in Lanzillotti's study. The giants told him that their price policies are designed to hold a particular share of the market, as well as a target rate of return. U.S. Steel executives said they wanted 30 percent of their market; Johns-Manville didn't want more than 20 percent of any market; International Harvester wanted "less than a dominant share" and General Electric, no more than 50 percent. This kind of self-imposed restraint is necessary if the system of peaceful price leadership is to survive and if the government is to keep its antitrust claws sheathed. An aggressive policy of price cutting to enlarge a slice of the market might wipe out weaker competitors but it would leave the leader exposed as a naked monopolist. Lanzillotti concluded: "Apparently the program of reach-

ing no more than a given market share and of moving ahead
against competition does not find expression in price reductions."

In less academic language, the system of target rates of
return and target market shares lifts prices and profits above
the level they would reach if the men in the executive suites
were forced into the perfectly competitive world of classical
economics.

In sum, modern corporate behavior resembles that of the
atomistic, Smithian firm about as much as a coach and four
does a jet airplane. But the consequences for the economy are
not nearly so smooth and efficient as this image suggests. In
the perfectly competitive mode, prices bear the force of
changes in demand. When demand for a product declines or
business generally slumps, prices drop. But in the modern
world of concentration and target pricing, production and
jobs bear the brunt of changes in demand. Prices in centralized industries are held more or less rigid or change slowly.

In the great depression of the 1930's, Gardiner Means
found that prices in the concentrated industries were cut very
little, but production and jobs were slashed drastically; in
contrast, in competitive sectors like agriculture and textiles,
prices fell sharply and employment and output were held up.
The fact of concentration, then, tends to hold back the economy's potential output and to increase unemployment. A
bizarre instance of this power over prices came in 1958 when
U.S. Steel and its followers actually raised prices near the
bottom of a business slump. If the industry had been forced
to behave in classical fashion, prices would have been cut,
more steel would have been produced and sold and more
jobs would have been created.

On the upswing, when the economy's demand is climbing,
the quest for stability also produces some peculiar effects. In
the competitive world, increased demand will lift prices; in
the world of concentration, however, a sharp rise in demand

will produce a much smaller rise in prices. If the demand is strong enough, the concentrated firms will be selling everything they can produce; demand will be pressing against industry's capacity. Then, instead of letting higher prices ration goods among the clamorous, well-heeled buyers, the industrial giants will set up their own arbitrary system of allocation. It won't be foolproof, however, and some of their production will find its way into higher-priced 'gray' markets. This is what happened in several concentrated industries after the end of World War II.

Concentration also tends to hold back innovation, the introduction of new machinery or technological change. At first glance, this seems surprising. Much business literature has insisted that the biggest firms are the most progressive, that advance comes from expensive research that only the giants can afford. This notion has become a part of conventional wisdom. But the logic of target pricing and the lure of security weaken the progressive strains of the giants. A big firm won't invest in a new process, a new machine or a new plant unless it promises to yield a return greater than the target.

For example, consider U.S. Polyglot and its target rate of 14 percent. A German firm develops a new and more efficient stamping machine that Polyglot might use. But if Polyglot figures that the machine will earn only 10 percent of its cost, Polyglot won't buy it. Not until a machine can earn 14 percent or more will it be worth Polyglot's while to invest. In other words, as long as target rates are above those that would exist in competitive markets, any innovation has a higher barrier to climb before it will be adopted by an industrial giant.

This is not merely a theoretical possibility. It is a commonplace of industrial life. The steel industry's belated introduction of the basic oxygen or LD furnace is a striking case in point. This technique for making steel was developed in

Austria in the early 1950's. It produces steel $5 to $9 a ton cheaper than the open hearth furnace. Moreover, the initial investment cost has been estimated at $18 to $23 a ton less than an open hearth. A firm using a basic oxygen furnace is also well equipped to adopt another process called continuous casting that eliminates some costly steps in conventional steel making. American firms, however, ignored the basic oxygen furnace all during the years that they were pushing prices up at a rapid rate. U.S. Steel, for example, does not plan to install its first until some time in 1964.

Why the long delay? The controller of Bethlehem Steel, Frank Brugler, explained it to a writer for *Fortune*. Brugler said, "We don't want to invest in a facility unless it will return, on the average, 20 percent before taxes operating at 60 to 70 percent of capacity." Another Bethlehem official added, "We move only when improvements are so good we can no longer afford what we've got."

In other words, pricing to reach a target return on a "normal" volume of output placed a tall hurdle in front of the efficient, cost-reducing European technique. American steelmakers spurned the new furnace until their exacting profit standards could be met.

It is commonly claimed that invention itself comes chiefly from the giants. This however is dubious. Prof. John Jewkes of Oxford traced the origin of 60 major twentieth century inventions and found that only a minority were developed by large firms. More than half were the product of individual inventors working without institutional backing. Their contributions included the gyro-compass, the first successful system of catalytic cracking, the jet engine, safety razor and the zipper. Small firms came up with cellophane and DDT among others. The high-powered and well-publicized research of the giants did bring such advances as nylon, tetraethyl lead, transistors and diesel electric motors. But in all, they accounted for a lesser share of the batch. Of course, the Jewkes list is a sample and does not measure the relative importance of each invention. But his study is suggestive. Taken together with the high profits barrier to innovation, it is likely that concentration and the existence of giant firms has impeded rather than advanced technological progress.

Another important consequence of concentration is the damage it does to the ideal distribution of rewards described in the harmonious world of textbook competition. In this elegant model, every actor in the economic drama is rewarded in accord with his contribution towards production. Each of the productive factors, the entrepreneur, the landowner, the laborer and the investor receives a profit, rent, wage or return that matches the value of his addition to the last commodity produced and sold in any industry. To be sure, this ideal never existed outside the pages of the texts. However, it embodies a powerful suggestion that impersonal justice tends to operate in the economic world.

In the real world of concentration, this logic is shattered and rewards can't be distributed in such a self-justifying fashion. One obvious example is the premium reward received by a stockholder of an industrial giant that has some power over its prices. In theory, stockholders are rewarded with dividends for supplying at some risk the capital of a corporation, the funds to pay for its investment in plants and machinery. Stockholders still fulfill this function for youthful, untested corporations. But the established industrial behemoth doesn't turn to its stockholders for financing. Instead, its investment is financed with what accountants call retained earnings. That is, U.S. Polyglot pays for its enlarged factories and new equipment largely out of its profits.

Polyglot, of course, gets these profits by selling its goods. Profits can be described simply as the difference between the cost of making a product and its price. So, it is Polyglot's customers who are actually supplying the capital with which Polyglot grows by paying the price that Polyglot charges. To be sure, the customers are supplying this capital involuntarily and not through any decision of their own. However, the yield or earnings from this increase in capital does not flow to Polyglot's customers. (Unless Polyglot is a regulated utility and a public commission insists that Polyglot give its customers a rebate of all profits above a competitive level.) Instead, some of the extra profits created by the new investment are distributed as dividends to Polyglot's stockholders. In effect, Polyglot is amassing from its customers what Representative Wright Patman of Texas has called "costless capital." Polyglot passes on the earnings of this capital to essentially passive stockholders who have risked no additional funds.*

One of the striking features of the 1962 steel price row was an argument, repeatedly advanced by Chairman Blough of U.S. Steel. He said that his company needed higher prices to pay for new, more modern equipment. In a competitive world, he would be unable to finance his investment from increased prices paid by his customers. He would be forced to raise new capital in competition with other firms, either through borrowing funds or by issuing new shares of stock. This is what regulated utilities must do because they are prohibited from making customers pay for their investment. In unregulated and concentrated manufacturing industries, however, the bulk of the money for new investment is supplied by consumers.†

Costless capital is one reason why managers of large cor-

---

* Because income from dividends (and wages) is taxed more heavily than stock market profits, many corporations hang on to a large portion of their extra profits from new investment. The stock market then regards this accumulation as an increase in the value of the stock shares and the shares tend to rise in price. So, the stockholders are not only in line for an unearned piece of cake; they can consume more of it than if the same slice came to them as dividends or wages.

† Since the end of World War II, corporations have financed from 70 percent to 83 percent of their investment out of their earnings. In 1962, for example, they raised $9.3 billion from the sale of stocks and bonds and $35.3 billion from profits and depreciation allowances. In other words, four of every five investment dollars came from the customers.

porations vote themselves handsome stock options in their own companies. These options give them the right to purchase shares in their companies for extended periods of time at prices near current levels. As a company's capital expands, thanks to its power over prices, the price of the stock tends to rise. Indeed, the existence of stock options is a powerful incentive for corporation managers to keep pushing up the prices of their products. The faster their company's stock rises, the wealthier the managers become. And as a frosting on this cake, rewards from the exercise of these options have been protected from the impact of ordinary income taxes.

Just as incomes are not distributed in the fashion prescribed by the classical texts, so too are resources improperly allocated in the world of concentration. In the classical model, labor, material resources and capital move at the price signals flashed by competitive markets to firms and industries where they are in greatest demand. So, resources are combined most efficiently in accord with consumer tastes. In the real world of concentration, industrial giants interfere with this smooth-working, automatic arrangement.

When business generally is slack, firms in concentrated industries tend to hold prices above the level that competition would set. As a result, they sell and produce less than consumers would take in a classical world. When business is booming, the opposite takes place. Concentrated industries then hold prices down and sell more than they would in the textbook setting.

The giants' objective of a stable market share probably distorts investment in another way, too. Harald Malmgren and Benjamin Caplan have called attention to this phenomenon. Say that Western Widgets, a follower in the concentrated widgets industry, decides to enlarge its capacity by erecting a new plant. The industry's price leader, General Widgets, will probably follow suit—not because of any increased demand for widgets but in order to preserve its share of the market. One or both factories will be partly unused unless General violates the code and cuts prices. It is more likely that widget customers will be hit with a price increase to pay for the new and idle plants.

Something like this has been happening in the American economy. Between 1958 and 1962, manufacturers spent $13.3 billion dollars a year for new investment. But during this period, 18 percent of their productive capacity was idle. Of course, much of the investment was designed to reduce costs rather than enlarge capacity. But some of it very likely stemmed from copycat strategy to hold on to a potential share of a market. These outlays distorted the proper mix between investment and consumption spending. Moreover, the very existence of excess idle capacity acts as a drag on the economy. When many plants are unused, corporations are less inclined to push ahead with new investment.

In contrast then with the watch-works world of classical economics, concentrated industries tend to push up prices, hold down production and employment, increase the barriers to technological progress, distort the flow of incomes and exert a distorting pull over the flow of resources.

The sluggish performance of the post-Korean War economy can be attributed in no small measure to the concentrated structure of business. To be sure, this sluggishness has occurred at a level high enough to enable many to live comfortably. There have been no deep depressions or massive unemployment like that of the 1930's or 1870's. The Keynesian lessons of World War II have not been entirely lost. Federal expenditures may not have been strong enough to create full employment but they have underwritten enough demand to prevent serious slumps and sustain some limited expansion. However, outlays for the Cold War have comprised an important part of the government's demand. Their abrupt removal could expose the economy to the full consequences of concentrated corporate policies. In the immediate future, there is considerable risk that the giants will undermine any more aggressive federal attack on the economy's ills. During the ten years following Korea, federal policy was often blunted by corporate pricing, investment and output decisions.

Both the Kennedy and the Eisenhower administrations sought a stable price level, high employment and a faster rate of growth in the output of goods and services. Both were frustrated to some extent because they employed broad-gauged policy tools that work best in a competitive economy.

Consider price policy. This was the central concern of the Eisenhower regime. In season and out, the Republican administration preached the doctrine of a stable price level and designed programs to focus on this objective. In the best classical fashion, officials reasoned that if the total demand for goods was held in check, prices could not rise. General Eisenhower and his Treasury secretaries tried to hold down demand by containing the increase in government expenditures; they encouraged the Federal Reserve System to sit on demand by restraining the volume of available credit. To their dismay, prices rose anyway. From 1953 to 1958, the wholesale price index climbed 8 percent.

Did the Republicans fail to clamp down hard enough on demand?

Some of them thought so, but they were clearly wrong. When demand is too exuberant in the classical world, all the economy's resources are employed. The extra, excessive demand must spill over to push up prices. But nothing like this happened in the Eisenhower era because this is not a classical world. Throughout the period during which prices were rising and demand was being checked, there were unemployed men and idle plants. Some experts, with considerable reason, complained that the Administration had clamped down so hard on demand that there wasn't enough of it to employ all the economy's resources. For the Eisenhower strategists, wedded to the textbook world, this was all very baffling.

From 1953 to 1958, the jobless rate for labor averaged 5 percent and for manufacturing plants, 15 percent. This was strong evidence that the Eisenhower administration had indeed sat on demand. Prices then must have been rising because of some other force. That force was exerted by the concentrated industries. Gardiner Means calculated that nearly seven-eighths of the price rise during the period had come from the concentrated industries where firms have the power to lift prices in the face of a sluggish demand. The Eisenhower restraints may have held back employment and growth; they did not curb the industrial giants.

The giants behaved in characteristic fashion, forcing production and employment to bear the burden of the restraints on demand. Unions in some of the concentrated industries strengthened this process. They demanded and received wage increases greater than the gains in their member's output. So, in order to merely maintain their target rates of return, corporations lifted their prices. In steel, the spiral went furthest. The best evidence, compiled by Means and the Senate Antitrust and Monopoly Subcommittee, indicates that the steelmakers were raising their target, increasing prices above the level needed to offset their higher labor costs.

Towards the end of the Eisenhower period and continuing in Kennedy's administration, the goal of a stable price level appeared to have been reached. From 1958 through 1962, the index of wholesale prices rose only one-quarter of one percent. But this stability was achieved at painful cost. During this time, the rate of unemployment climbed higher, averaging nearly 6 percent.

The position, then, has been about like this. In the earlier Eisenhower years, there was considerable unemployment and rising prices. In the later Eisenhower and the Kennedy years, there was more unemployment and stable prices. Neither administration could combine high employment with a steady price level. This is just what might be expected in a world in which large firms can and do lift their prices above competitive levels.

Both administrations also worried about new industrial investment. They agreed that increased spending for new machinery would stimulate faster economic growth. The Kennedy administration created an array of tax magnets to attract enlarged corporate investment. But here again, the industrial giants tend to weaken the pull of this lure. They weaken it in two ways. Because their target rates are above competitive profit levels, the giants demand a premium return on any new investment. So they will respond less strongly than classical competitors to any tax inducement. Moreover, the giants' pricing policies limit output and jobs. This means that the potential market for all goods is curbed. Since companies invest primarily to serve expanding markets, the limits imposed on these markets by price policies shrink the attractiveness of new technology. The Kennedy investment tax credit, bigger depreciation allowances and lower corporate income levies will probably induce some spending for machinery that would not otherwise have been made. But it is likely that this extra investment will be less than it would have been in a world of classical competitors.

The other Kennedy programs to strengthen the economy also run a serious risk of veto from the pricing policies of concentrated industries. The Administration, it will be recalled, had decided to stimulate demand openly by cutting taxes and covertly by letting military expenditures rise. But the quickening of demand caused by these policies may well encourage large corporations to raise their prices as the steel industry did again in 1963. The extra demand that the federal programs should supply would then be eroded. Instead of enlarging the demand for goods and creating more jobs, the tax-freed dollars and the extra federal outlays would be eaten up by higher costs. It is not likely that this will take place on a matching basis with price increases erasing all of the additional demand. But the effectiveness of the Kennedy stimulants depends to a remarkable extent on the price behavior of the dominant corporations.

If concentration saps the economist's policies, it also raises some disturbing questions for political theorists. A democratic society assumes that power and responsibility are linked. The exercise of power in government is legitimate when officials are ultimately responsible for their actions to a sovereign people who can and do replace them. The problem of legitimacy does not arise in Adam Smith's world, for no producer in a competitive market has any power over price, output and investment. Each responds to the dictates of a sovereign market. But in a world of concentrated industries, the large corporations enjoy considerable discretion and they exercise an important share of economic sovereignty.

Indeed, their power extends directly to areas that are usually regarded as the exclusive preserve of the state. The large international corporations literally create a portion of American foreign policy. The investment, pricing and production decisions of Standard Oil Co. (N.J.) in Venezuela or Saudi Arabia are an integral element of national policy overseas. The operations of General Motors in France, United Fruit in Central America or Firestone in Liberia not only condition but are part of the stuff of relations with foreign nations.

"What all this seems to add up to," Edward Mason of Harvard concludes, "is the existence of important centers of private power in the hands of men whose authority is real but whose responsibilities are vague."

Where are the sanctions for the prices these giants set?

What forces guide their investment and output decisions? Freed to a considerable if immeasurable extent of the restraints of competitive markets, to whom must they answer? The standard reply in business literature is the stockholder. But even if this were true, why should it be so? The typical stockholder is no longer supplying capital out of his savings to competitive firms struggling in markets they can't dominate. For the large corporation, the stockholder is, as we have seen, a passive actor in the industrial drama. It is the customers who supply most of the capital.

In any case, stockholders are not likely to grumble over the actions of corporate managers unless the value of their shares is seriously threatened. Even then, the shareholders are usually impotent. While the ownership of stocks is concentrated in a relatively narrow band of the population, ownership in any single large corporation is fragmented. Because of the diffusion of stock ownership in each major corporation, the managers become a largely self-perpetuating group. Indeed the managers' grip on the machinery that elects corporate directors is so firm that a fight for control of all but the sleepiest giants is unthinkable. As Professor Kaysen has said, "The power of corporate management is, in the political sense, irresponsible power, answerable ultimately only to itself."

Despite the worshipful hymns sung by and for the great corporations, there is nothing sacred or immutable about the business structure. It was not, after all, created in a burst of divine inspiration but is the product of a long evolution. The private corporation is merely one response to the modern world's technological demand for large aggregations of capital. The business structure, like any other institutional arrangement, is a means to an end.

The obvious purpose of an economic order is the provision of increasing material welfare, of a growing stock of widely distributed goods and services. Less apparent is the implicit demand that many make and this inquiry supports, that the economy should provide a setting which encourages the maximum play for the potential abilities of individual men. The concentrated American economy, however, tends to frustrate both ends. How can the structure be re-ordered to further these purposes without impairing either?

An analysis of possible solutions could range over the entire body of political and economic thought since the early nineteenth century. But no such grandiose exercise needs to be undertaken here. Unsatisfactory as the economy's performance has been, it is clear that current economic problems are not so overwhelming in character as to license radical solutions. The more extreme statist remedies, nationalizing key industries or the means of production generally, are obviously irrelevant to the American setting. Whether they involve a benign democratic socialism or a malignant totalitarianism, such heroic expedients need not be entertained seriously because the American plight is simply not so desperate. Most importantly, the problem of freedom in a state economy can't be dissolved with the simple assurance that there is no problem since the people and state are one. The visibly stifling bureaucracies of the Communist world have robbed this innocent notion of its virginity.

But there is a range of alternatives, much less drastic and much closer to the American tradition. One is an extension of public utility regulation. This is the typical framework for industries like power, transportation, and communications. These are industries in which competition appears to be wasteful or destructive.

Should public commissioners sit in judgment on the decisions of the giant corporations in other major industries? Some giants clearly regard themselves as quasi-utilities despite their public rhetoric about the glories of free, competitive enterprise. After discussions with U.S. Steel executives, Lanzillotti concluded that the company's management regards itself as "vested with the responsibility and subject to the inhibitions of a public utility." The technique of setting targets to obtain satisfactory—not maximum—profits is a public utility approach.

Regulation by commission, however, raises more problems than it solves. What criteria will guide the regulators of, say, the auto industry? How will they determine what is the appropriate price, model style, output, investment, employment and the like? Even if agreement could be reached on some proper rate of profits, what incentive would there be for a General Motors to reduce costs, to innovate, if all its savings simply resulted in a commission order to lower prices.

If the regulators exercised genuine and ultimate control, there is also a danger that they would cramp the regulated industries. Bureaucracies prefer routine. To be sure, bureaucracy is as much a characteristic of the giant corporation as it is of government agencies. But the authoritarian industrial bureaucracy is probably more flexible, better able to adapt to change than its government counterpart.

The history of the regulated industries is not very comforting. Even in the absence of outright corruption, and this is common enough, the regulatory board has typically become the captive of the industry it is supposed to oversee. This subject is explored in more detail in Chapter 5. But this blunt summary by Professor Adams appears close to the mark: "Public regulation, originally designed to protect the public interest, is transformed into a system of privilege, protection, and subsidy for private monopoly."

Perhaps the greatest weakness of utility regulation and its variants is that it is a piecemeal affair. The rules and orders for one industry are issued in a vacuum, largely unrelated to their consequences for other industries and other sectors of the economy. Indeed, no coherence is possible because the regulators are not guided by a meaningful comprehensive objective. Commissioners of even the greatest integrity and acumen face the same problem as men of lesser stuff. They are generally given no more specific mandate than to further the public interest. This is a noble end but it obviously lacks precision. Unless the regulated industries are linked together in some coherent scheme, the likelihood of contradiction, cross-purpose and confusion is great.

Since economists have invested so heavily in the competitive model, many of them long to recreate a Smithian world in fact. So a second possible solution is advanced by many scholars (although it is little more than a ritual incantation for most). This is the demand for more vigorous use of the antitrust laws, breaking up the giant complexes and establishing the sanctions of competition by legislative and judicial fiat. The tougher-minded trust busters are well aware that contemporary technology requires large companies in many industries. To erect a steel plant, an electrical machinery factory or an auto assembly line takes sizeable amounts of capital. The economists, of course, don't want to destroy the gains in productive efficiency that large aggregates can yield. However, the trust busters contend that there are few if any economic gains achieved by grouping more or less similar plants under one corporate shell. In their view, a Big Three could be reduced to a medium-sized thirty or forty with no loss in technological efficiency and enormous gains in competitive behavior.

The courts, however, have been reluctant to break up going concerns, to unscramble the corporate egg, particularly in the absence of conspiratorial price-fixing or some other gross misbehavior. So some of the trust busters have proposed amending the antitrust laws. One of the more thoughtful suggestions in this vein has come from Kaysen and Turner. They would break up into viable, separate concerns any corporation exercising "unreasonable" market power. "Unreasonable" power would be defined arbitrarily. Its existence would be assumed, whenever one concern accounts for perhaps half or more of an industry's sales or four firms account for at least 80 percent. The giants could escape division if they showed that their pre-eminence arose as the result of gains in efficiency, or from patented inventions or innovations, or if the economic costs of a break-up would be too great.

Again, however, the history of antitrust legislation is not inspiring. The existing laws may have slowed down but have certainly not diminished concentration. Indeed, the first great merger wave that created many of the present giants came in the decade following the birth of the original law, the Sherman Act of 1890. Similarly, the second great burst of mergers in the 1920's took place after the passage of the second great antitrust law, the Clayton Act of 1914. And the third era of corporate consolidation got under way just as Congress in 1950 was enacting the Celler-Kefauver amendment to close a gaping Clayton Act loophole.

The antitrust approach puts a great burden on the government agencies filing complaints and on the courts. Both branches have generally resisted using antitrust laws for a wholescale reordering of the economy's structure. Instead, the laws have been employed as a partial check on further concentration. In recent years, the government has acted to prevent or undo some mergers. But it rarely files a suit to break up a going corporation. Characteristically, the Kennedy administration indicated that it would limit antitrust powers to a policeman's job, striking at conspiracy and other forms of misconduct.

However, what has been need not necessarily be. The Kaysen-Turner proposal and similar ideas deserve more attention. Whether they get it depends in great measure on the extent of public concern over the distortions in the economy and the threat to democratic practice posed by the giant corporations. But even if new life is pumped into trust busting, the world of perfect competition won't be created. Twenty-five sizeable firms in an industry will behave more like classical competitors than five. However, they will still retain some discretion over prices. They will take account of each other's moves unlike the archetypal farmer in the impersonal market. Moreover, it would take years to reshape the business structure with a trenchant antitrust program. The Congress and the executive branch are unlikely to move this side of a crisis. If and when they do, the unraveling process would take a long time to work itself out in the courts. Most of all, there is the disposition, already noted, to let sleeping antitrust laws lie.

For these reasons, there has been a recent and growing interest in proposals to retain the existing business structure but harness it more firmly to social ends.

Gardiner Means, who has explored so much of the wilderness of concentration, advanced a novel idea. He has suggested giving bonuses for good behavior to managers of the giants. An open admirer of the large corporations, he would keep the technique of target pricing but induce managers to choose socially desirable target rates of return. The socially desirable rate would be linked to the competitive cost for capital. For example, electric utilities now must raise their capital funds from the public. Assume that they pay six percent for this cash. Means figures that a riskier manufacturing corporation would be entitled to something more than this, perhaps eight or nine percent. The large corporation should then set its prices to earn this rate on a normal volume. Its managers would receive bonuses of varying amounts depending on several factors: their ability to reach the target in normal business conditions, to earn more in boom times and less in slump periods and on their skill in reducing costs through innovations. The bonuses would be taxed at less than the usual rates, much like the tax-privileged stock options that managers have been voting themselves.

This ingenious idea, however, suffers from some of the same flaws embodied in utility regulation. Ultimately some government agency, perhaps the Treasury, would have to pass on the bonus systems, determining their qualifications for tax benefits. Without the free play of market forces, how could these officials fix the appropriate criteria for bonus-worthy production, investment and innovation? In time, wouldn't this agency accept whatever the managers proposed, much as the regulatory agencies now do? And again, bonus systems contrived separately for each concentrated industry would suffer from a lack of integration around a common objective. If bonuses for the electrical machinery industry, for example, stimulated rapid growth while those for electric power executives were geared to stability, the resulting imbalance and distortion would be costly.

Another and simpler proposal, a cousin to utility regulation, was put forward by the late Senator Joseph O'Mahoney of Wyoming, and has been revived in a bill by Senator Joseph Clark of Pennsylvania and Representative Henry Reuss of Wisconsin. It has attracted a scattering of support, generally from more militant liberals. This approach would compel major corporations in prominent, concentrated industries to defend any proposed price increase before a public board. The board would hold open hearings and examine the corporation's officers. If the corporation cited increased wage costs as the reason for the increase, their union would be subjected to the inquiry. The board would then issue a report and recommendations and so try to mobilize public opinion behind a course of price or wage action. However, after the report has been published, the corporation would be free to raise its prices.

This proposal has several obvious merits. If corporations were forced to rationalize their conduct under a public spotlight, their behavior might be more enlightened. The whole approach leaves private decision makers with considerable freedom, a desirable end in itself. But there are clear drawbacks, too. A corporation defying the board's recommendation would invite the very regulation that the technique seeks to avoid. Again, on what basis would the board act? Where are the criteria to guide its recommendation? Like Means' idea, the public hearing approach lacks standards. The procedure, moreover, would be cumbersome. It would force the delay of decisions that, from an economic standpoint, ought to be taken promptly. Moreover, it would destroy much of the remaining incentive to reduce prices. A corporation might achieve a great advance in efficiency that would induce it to cut a price. But if it had to justify future price increases at a public hearing, it would be tempted to forego the possible price cut and bank the savings in costs for a later day. Moreover, the hearing board deals with only one element in the corporate equation, price (and therefore, profits). It does not touch the second driving wheel of corporate action, the objective of holding a given market share. And this objective, like price policy, has important consequences for investment, production and employment decisions. Finally, without some specific over-all set of objectives, the hearing boards like utility commissions would be making decisions on a piecemeal basis.

Another technique that was once discussed but has now dropped out of sight might well be looked at again. This is the creation of the yardstick firm. A government steel plant, electrical machinery producer or auto company might have the same limiting effect on prices and the same liberating effect on services as the Tennessee Valley Authority power plants have had on private utilities. Again, however, these government factories would require sophisticated accounting by dedicated officials of an extremely high order.

Still another route has been attempted in Western Europe and Japan, the system of indicative or noncoercive planning.

This has been one of the genuinely creative political inventions of the postwar world and its development has paralleled a remarkable prosperity in the economies that have turned to it. Indicative planning, little known in the United States, deserves closer examination and is discussed at length in the final chapter.

At this point, it is apparent that there are no panaceas, no simple solutions. The problem of reconciling technical efficiency, full use of resources, an equitable distribution of the fruits of potential abundance and maximum freedom probably demands compromise. If no single formula fits, why shouldn't a pragmatic society experiment with several at once? The steel industry, for example, appears to be an obvious target for deconcentration, for division into more competitors. Hearing boards might be appropriate for automobiles. A government chemical plant could provide a yardstick for measuring private performance and inducing new courses of action.

Admittedly, the prospects for experiment are dubious. Concentration and its consequences rank near the bottom of the public and the scholarly agendas. A society in which three-fifths are either affluent or have reasonable expectations of becoming so cannot be expected to show much interest in transforming its structure. Moreover, the prevailing mood of self-satisfaction has been reinforced in recent years by a curious doctrine of neopaternalism. Its theme is simple: concentration exists but there is no need for alarm. The managers of the modern giants are vastly different from their robber baron antecedents. The new managers are professionals, responsible men with a social conscience. In this view, power exists but is exercised so skillfully that it should not be disturbed. A world of abundance is indeed at hand; let these socially responsible managers lead us into it. How well this seductive theory fits the facts requires some special attention.

4. Of Consciences and Kings

> If the company of scholars who compose the Graduate School of Business Administration are men who feel its rightness as being part of *God's* eternal purpose in the evolution of mankind, who can question its future success?
> —Douglas Horton, Dean emeritus, Harvard Divinity School

IN AN EARLIER and simpler age, the moral behavior of businessmen was largely the concern of theologians. In the economists' view, each man's hand could and should be turned against every other's, or so the theory ran. For out of this jungle where each pursues his own self-interest, the maximum well-being of all would be obtained. This doctrine of the classical economists rested on a crucial assumption, the assumption of perfect competition. But in the modern economy, industries are typically organized around a few competitors, each forced to take account of the others' decisions and all possessing some degree of discretion. In such an economy, narrow self-interest does not insure a state of bliss; decisions lack the automatic sanction of Adam Smith's invisible hand. Thoughtful businessmen and business commentators have fully grasped this theoretical deficiency; to fill the gap they have proclaimed the existence of a new breed of managers whose decisions are guided by a profound sense of social responsibility.

This "managerial creed," as one scholarly examination de-

scribed it, asserts that "the evil days of rugged individualism
have now passed and that a new era of business responsibility
has emerged."

The new doctrine of legitimacy attempts to make a virtue
of necessary fact and, in more or less unflinching fashion,
confronts the reality of the impotent shareholder. At its simplest, the argument goes like this: In the giant corporation,
owners and managers are two distinct groups. The large concerns are legally owned by tens of thousands of stockholders.
no one of them controlling enough shares to exert any decisive
influence over the firm's destiny. Because of this diffusion of
ownership, the typical corporation is run by a largely self-
perpetuating group of office-managers. Their control of the
machinery through which corporate directors are elected and
the high cost of rounding up enough shares to oust them in a
proxy fight, give the managers an almost impregnable position. However, this is a good thing. It frees the managers
from the parochial interest of the shareholders in share prices
and dividends; it enables the managers to carefully balance
the claims of all groups in society. The typical chairman or
president of the modern corporation is a professional manager, trained in a school of business administration to strike
this proper balance.

An early formulation of the new creed was enunciated in
1928 by Owen D. Young, the chairman of the General Electric Co. He said:

> We have come to consider [these managers as] trustees of
> the whole undertaking, whose responsibility is to see to it on
> the one side that the invested capital is safe and its return is
> adequate and continuous; and on the other side that compe-
> tent and conscientious men are found to do the work and that
> their job is safe and their earnings are adequate and continu-
> ous.

A more elaborate version was promulgated in 1962 by the executives of corporate, theological and educational institutions who sat on the Business Ethics Advisory Council of the Secretary of Commerce. They said:

> Every business enterprise has manifold responsibilities to the society of which it is a part. The prime legal and social obligation of the managers of a business is to operate it for the long-term profit of its owners. Concurrent social responsibilities pertain to a company's treatment of its past, present and prospective employees and to its various relationships with customers, suppliers, government, the community, and the public at large.

The prophets of the new creed are not always clear whether corporate executives should strive for this state of grace or whether they have already attained it. Sometimes, the apostles say they are describing what is; sometimes, they are urging what ought to be. The editors of Henry Luce's *Fortune* magazine, in their *U. S. A.: The Permanent Revolution*, betray this confusion.

At one point, they assert that "Big Business, if only because it is subject to the most pressure, exercises its power with a strong and growing sense of responsibility." However, twenty pages on, this becomes a mere belief or theory. The editors declare that "the old concept that the owner has a right to use his property just the way he pleases has evolved into the belief that ownership carries social obligations, and that a manager is a trustee not only for the owner but for society as a whole."

No such ambiguity troubles David Lilienthal. In his *Big Business: A New Era*, he heralds the arrival of a "new kind of 'top boss' of large business undertakings." The new boss possesses "a strong and practical sense of responsibility to the public and an awareness of the ethics of present-day business competition."

A more sophisticated version, flyspecked with qualifications, is found in Adolph A. Berle's *The Twentieth Century Capitalist Revolution*. With Gardiner Means, Berle first drew attention in 1932 to the crucial divorce between corporate ownership and management. He argues that the corporations are leading the way to a modern "City of God" because their managers are tending to respond to the promptings of conscience or some inchoate higher law. Berle suggests that powerful corporate managers have little choice but to take account of the good life in their decision making. If they don't, he warns, the state will supersede them and make the decisions instead.

Berle openly worries about the lack of an institutional conscience in corporations, a mechanism designed to insure that the "City of God" will be considered in their deliberations. But in another essay, he flatly declares that the conscience is functioning anyway. He says, "The principles and practices of big business in 1959 seem to me considerably more responsible, more perceptive and (in plain English) more honest than they were in 1929. The methods, morals and social education of the leaders of big business actually seem to have improved substantially in a generation."

The prophets of the moral revolution in the executive suite do not claim modern managers to be a divinely inspired elite. Such a notion would leave too much to chance, too much to the supernatural. Instead, functional explanations are provided for the new redemption. Some of the prophets stress the force of public opinion. Large corporations, it is argued, are under a constant, searching public spotlight. If they misbehave, it will go hard with them, for an aroused citizenry will turn to the state to punish them. Sometimes the prophets underline the power of the other groups whose claims the managers must balance. Organized labor, large customers, groups of dealers, the government itself are all aggregates of power, it is asserted. Their pressure and potential power to retaliate guarantees the responsible conduct of the new managers.

Schools of business administration occupy a strategic role in this scheme. They are the spawning grounds of the Big Organization men, they impart the techniques and values that train commonplace undergraduates for a life of responsible service in the corporate temple. Berle observes that "at least two great business schools—Harvard and Columbia—have offered programs of background information and thinking in the larger ranges of social organization to selected business executives." And this is one of the forces that is creating, he says, "a body of sophisticated thinking whose aim, properly analyzed, is a conception of a community making for the good life."

Because of this vital, seminarian role, let us examine the scripture according to the most prominent business school, the one at Harvard. A cursory examination of the 1962–63 catalogue confirms the school's concern with the moral revolution. Its 116 pages contain at least eight separate references to right conduct.

A student at the Harvard University Graduate School of Business Administration, we are told, "develops a concept of ethical values and of social responsibility in the making of concrete business decisions." Elsewhere, the catalogue is sprinkled with phrases like the "responsibility that business leaders have to society" and "the responsibilities of business to the American society as a whole."

Harvard's Divinity School, older and perhaps less optimistic, does not claim as much.

At this point, a sceptic might complain that the *Fortune* editors, Lilienthal, Berle and the authors of the business school catalogue are somewhat vague. Their sentiments may be unexceptional, but they lack concreteness. How exactly do corporate managers determine when a decision is socially responsible? What are their standards and how are they derived? How are competing claims measured and weighed in the boardrooms? If backsliding occurs, what recourse does society have?

A close look at the one course devoted entirely to these considerations might provide some answers. This is the half-year course entitled "Business, Society and the Individual," or BSI in the acronymic world of embryo corporate executives.

"The primary concern of this course," the catalogue tells us, "is realistic managerial decision making in business situations in a private enterprise economy which requires profit, and which is complicated by the presence of issues of public responsibility, fairness, integrity, right and wrong, personal conscience."

BSI, like "Creative Marketing Strategy" or "Factory Management" is an optional course offered to second-year students. Unfortunately, it was not given in 1962–63 because the professor, George Albert Smith, Jr., was on leave in Switzerland. However, he left behind his own text, 762 pages of documents and cases that his students would have studied if he had been in Cambridge.

Professor Smith's personal position is clear in general if not in particular. In an introductory essay, he says: "Business and other leaders today more than ever must take into account in their decisions the good of society as a whole." Since corporate managers are largely self-selecting, they have "not only great power but a great burden of responsibility." And, "I believe businessmen themselves are morally accountable for the use they make of the human and material resources under their control."

The heart of the Harvard Business School's method is the case system, the study of situations drawn from the actual

world of business. Professor Smith's cases range over a bigger
territory than salesman Willy Loman dreamed of.

Some pose rather simple, Sunday School issues of honesty.
Should a dealer in motor scooters who divides promotion expenses with his distributor, permit his advertising agency to
pad the bills in order to shrink his share of the costs? Should
a business school student, offered an expense-paid trip for a
job interview by two different firms in the same city, collect
his expenses twice?

Some of the cases raise broader questions of responsibility.
How should the steel executives respond to President Kennedy's request for price restraint? Should a candy manufacturer with a plant in the Philippines introduce machinery that
would lay off half his work force? Should a producer of carbon
black sell his product or license his knowledge to the Soviet
Union?

There are, of course, no textbook solutions to these questions. George Smith does not profess to be a Solomon. Nor
does he claim to be a new Adam Smith, developing a theory
that provides ready answers for decision makers. Near the end
of his text, George Smith quotes another business school
scholar, Richard Eells of Columbia, who says:

"The well-tempered corporation is a system of private government with *self-generated* principles of constitutionalism
that match corporate authority to corporate responsibilities
and impose restraints upon corporate officialdom for the protection of the rights of persons and property against abuse of
corporate power."

Thus, Eells, who has also been in charge of something
called "public policy research" at General Electric, lets the cat
out of the bag. He ends up where the catalogue began. The
principles of responsible corporate behavior cannot be expli-
cated. They are "self-generating" or, in effect, somehow di-
vined. Both Smith of Harvard and Eells of Columbia, it is

safe to say, would be dismayed at the suggestion that these principles can be discovered by studying the entrails of sacrificial chickens. However, there is no reason to believe that this method is any less fruitful than a close study of BSI.

Indeed, a plausible reading of Smith's cases suggests that the course is essentially a primer, introducing students to the kinds of pressures that will hamper their power when they reach the executive suite. The classroom discussions of the cases probably produce some ingenious rationales for harsh decisions. The one Harvard course dealing directly with the social responsibility of businessmen may teach less about welfare decision making than about manipulating possible adversary groups like government, labor, consumers and suppliers.

Whatever the gap between BSI's proclaimed and actual purpose, there is no warrant for a cynical evaluation of businessmen themselves. If theory, Berle and the Harvard Business School can't supply answers, this does not mean the corporate executives are not genuinely concerned about the gulf between their power and its sanction, between their performance and their aspirations.

In 1961, Reverend Raymond C. Baumhart, a Jesuit priest and former student at the Business School, sent a provocative questionnaire to 5000 readers of the Harvard Business Review. Seventeen hundred replied and of these, nearly three-quarters described themselves as members of either "top management" or "middle management." Nearly half said they agreed with a statement that American businessmen tend to ignore ethical laws and are preoccupied chiefly with gain; four of seven thought that businessmen would breach a code of ethics if they figured they could get away with it; four of five said there are practices generally accepted in their own industry which they personally regarded as unethical. Among these generally accepted unethical practices they cited: lavish entertaining to seek favors; kickbacks to customers' purchasing agents; price fixing and misleading advertising.

These replies do not reflect a world of amoral executives, accepting the business life for what it is; instead, Reverend Baumhart's respondents display a marked uneasiness about their own role and that of their fellows. The late Professor Benjamin M. Selekman of the Harvard Business School once declared: "Outside of church circles, I find nowhere so much moral ferment as among corporation executives and teachers of business."

Mencken would have scoffed at that but Sinclair Lewis might have agreed. If "ferment" means distress and confusion, then Selekman's observation is reinforced by Reverend Baumhart's questionnaire. The point is this: there is nothing in the logic or practice of concentrated corporate industries that guides or compels socially responsible decision making. Moreover, the very determination of what is a responsible decision and who is to be held responsible is neither simple nor clear. There is no formula that explains how competing claims are to be gratified; there is no theory that fixes responsibility on specific actors in the corporate drama.

In the style of the Business School, let us examine a few cases that illustrate the difficulties confronting the concept of responsible executives.

Few corporations are more admired than the giant General Electric Co., in sales the fourth ranking industrial corporation in 1960. As Berle said, "The General Electric Company is, justly, one of the most respected of American corporations. Its management has been able and of unquestioned integrity."

GE of course was the kingpin of the greatest criminal price conspiracy known to the antitrust laws.

High ranking officials in GE and other electrical machinery producers met secretly to agree on and sometimes raise prices and allocate shares of markets. The conspiracies—and there

were many, separate ones—ranged from giant turbine-genera-
tors to small watt hour meters. They embraced several billions
of dollars in sales. The business executives resorted to tricks
drawn from stereotyped thriller movies to hide their tracks.
They communicated in plain, unmarked envelopes, called
each other only from public telephones, and invented exotic
formulas like the "phase of the moon" to rotate business
among themselves.

GE's central role was underlined by its share of the penal-
ties ultimately imposed. Of the 20 indictments brought by the
government, GE was involved in 19; it pleaded guilty to 6
and unwilling to contest to 13 others. Of the seven executives
who served brief jail sentences, three came from GE, including a vice-president and two general managers. Eight other
GE officials were given suspended sentences; another five were
fined. The corporation itself paid $437,500 in fines of the
$1,924,500 assessed on the 29 companies.

The government charged that the conspiracies began as
early as 1951. However, Clarence E. Burke, general manager
of GE's switchgear and control division, testified he had been
"initiated" in 1945; William S. Ginn, the jailed vice president, said he discovered price fixing in the industry as early
as 1938 or 1939; and Robert Paxton, GE's president, said he
had learned of price fixing at least as early as the middle
1930's.

In fact, GE has been running afoul of the antitrust laws for
half a century. Between 1911 and 1952, the company had
been ordered to abandon some illicit practices or been convicted or pleaded nolo contendere in thirteen separate alleged
breaches of the monopoly laws. In sum, the remarkable cases
to which GE pleaded guilty in 1960 were neither isolated
incidents nor a sudden irruption of erratic behavior. However,
the corporation itself and its chief officers have repeatedly
insisted that they were not accountable for the illegal acts of

their subordinates. A few of the conspirators and some out-
siders suggested that the GE's very mode of existence induced
law-breaking. GE's leaders denied this as vigorously as they
rejected any imputation of personal responsibility.

Who then was responsible? In the view of GE's highest
management, only those who had directly participated in the
conspiracy. And why was this so? Simply because GE had cir-
culated a directive instructing its executives to obey antitrust
laws and not to engage in agreements or discussions with competitors over prices and other competitive matters.

A typical view was expressed by the immediate superior of
the convicted executives. Arthur F. Vinson, who rejoiced in
the titles of "Group Executive" and "Vice President," was in
charge of the three GE divisions that were shot through with
illegal price-fixing. But he was sure no serious blame should
attach to him.

The Senate Antitrust and Monopoly Subcommittee ques-
tioned Vinson about his relation to the conspirators.

"It was my duty," he said, "to have trustworthy, capable
management in place and I delegated that authority and de-
pended on them to do this job."

At another point, Vinson pictured himself as a sort of phi-
losopher, aloof from the hurly-burly of prices and sales. He
said, ". . . it is my job to coach, guide and help and be
knowledgeable to the extent that you can . . ."

At most, he would acknowledge some flaw in his Socratic
dialogue. Vinson concluded his testimony by saying, "I think
we could do a better teaching job" on antitrust matters. "Perhaps we didn't do enough talking about it."

On the next rung of the corporate ladder stood President
Robert Paxton. In his view "a handful of people" had "de-
parted from proper conduct." He, himself, could be blamed
only for "an unsuccessful supervision." The guilty handful,
he said, "were supposed to be mature businessmen. They are

supposed to be responsible businessmen. They are supposed
to be people who conduct themselves properly."

Paxton had preceded Vinson directly in charge of the
tainted divisions before he moved up to the presidency. But
he insisted that GE's troubles flowed from some black lambs
who had strayed from the fold because of their earlier, pre-GE
rearing; neither the shepherds nor the sheep pen were faulty.

Paxton told the Senators, "Too much of the morality of
the business life has to be taught by the employer. It should
have been taught by a church; it should have been taught by
a school; and above all things, it should have been taught at
home, but it isn't."

The highest executive at GE, Chairman Ralph J. Cordiner,
at first adopted a somewhat ambiguous stance before the Subcommittee. He said, "As chief executive officer, I accept my
share of responsibility for what happened, even though I did
not know of these secret violations of the law or condone such
acts."

But under questioning, it became clearer that Cordiner regarded his "share of responsibility" as minute and he returned
to the Vinson-Paxton thesis of a corrupt few. The GE chairman said: ". . . finally this comes down to the individual
attitude of an individual person and how responsive they are
to the teaching and the belief and the conviction."

Senator Roman Hruska of Nebraska asked Cordiner what
he thought of a bill that would punish the head of a company
who had failed to preach compliance with antitrust laws and
whose subordinates had then violated the laws.

Cordiner replied, "I don't quite know how you could consistently in this country have this peculiar type of penalty on
an individual that didn't either do it, know about it, or condone it."

Hruska, who may not have read Berle or Selekman, observed approvingly: ". . . after all, this man is not a white

father. He is not even God. He can't know everything nor can he vouch for everybody in his company, 240,000 of them . . ."

If Cordiner was fuzzy about his responsibility before the senators, he was a little sharper in a speech he gave to GE officials at Hot Springs, Virginia on the eve of the first 1960 indictments.

"A man who is general manager," he said, referring to several executives whose heads were later to roll, "has tremendous ethical responsibilities. He must also be held accountable for his own performance and the performance of his component . . . With authority and responsibility goes accountability and measurement. I hold all officers and general managers and managers accountable and responsible for violation of this (antitrust) policy on the part of any individual in any component for which they have accountability, in accordance with their assigned responsibility and authority."

This made it clear that Cordiner did not regard himself as derelict in any way, for he was holding others responsible. However, his obscure reference to the accountability of "officers" sounds as if he was considering some punishment for Vinson and Paxton. In time, the tainted divisions were shifted out from under Vinson but new ones were put in their place. Paxton resigned after the company and its executives were sentenced. But the official reason given was Paxton's poor health.

As a corporate entity, GE was as emphatic as Cordiner that guilt lay elsewhere. In a report designed to provide GE's management with the company line, the firm's lawyers said that "their instinctive reaction" was that it "appeared tragic" that GE "should be held responsible for the acts of a handful of managers who had betrayed their trust."

And in the 1960 annual report to stockholders, GE declared:

"The Company pleaded nolo contendere to 13 of these indictments, while pleading guilty to six others upon being advised by counsel that the Company may be held *technically responsible* [my emphasis] for the acts of its employees even when they have violated a clear, long-standing Company Directive Policy setting up standards of conduct more stringent than requirements of the antitrust laws."

Responsibility, in this view, is individual and personal: it is neither executive nor corporate. But if this is so, what happens to the doctrine of responsible executives?

Lilienthal suggests that responsible executives are made, not born, in the corporate mold. At one point in his panegyric to the new era, he declares that industrial management is recognizing that its task "is not only to produce a good product at a profit, but to develop people" and that "people do not develop and grow unless they are given responsibility . . ." So he beams approvingly on the deeds and words of a then fresh GE president who had recently broken down his centralized corporation to give subordinates more authority. The new president was Cordiner.

But if these subordinates, given greater responsibility, fail to grow and develop in accord with the Lilienthal-Cordiner plan, is it because the organization pursues other goals and practices that conflict with its character-building program? Some of the convicted executives said as much.

When Lewis J. Burger, a GE general manager, appeared before the federal court to be sentenced for his part in the price conspiracy, his lawyer contended that GE's higher executives had subjected Burger to unhealthy pressure. The attorney observed that Burger had inherited a going conspiracy when he was promoted to manage GE's switchgear and control division.

"It was commented to him," the lawyer said, "that his predecessor had performed well, and it was added to Mr.

Burger that he was at risk. This meant, sir, that unless he proved himself within a two-year period of time he would be forced to leave the company . . . quite literally, it meant that he would depart from the General Electric Co."

Burger's attorney was suggesting that his client had been given an implicit order to duplicate the illegal behavior of his predecessor.

Another jailed GE executive, Vice President Ginn, also suggested that the top management had been ruthless. Senator Estes Kefauver asked Ginn if the company's stress on increased profits was one factor in breeding conspiracies.

Ginn replied, "Yes; I think this is right. I think the question of trying to get more business and to get more profits—and this I am perfectly willing to criticise my former employer for. I think that we had some economic pressures here of trying to increase the percentage available and your profits all at the same time, and it can't necessarily be done . . . I think the pressure is still there."

But Chairman Cordiner vigorously denied that GE's market share and profit targets had led the guilty executives astray.

"I was there and would have been quite aware if there had been that kind of pressure disproportionately applied on any of these gentlemen," he said. "I would refer you to the fact that all of these other areas of the company did not respond to this sort of a situation from anything that we presently know."

The wrongdoing, Cordiner reiterated was personal, not institutional; it arose from defects of character, not contradictions in GE. The guilty officials, he said, had succumbed to the temptations of "a very human desire to have power control" and to "a lazy, indolent way of doing business as against all-out, hard-hitting competition."

This is precisely the point. In many of the company's "other areas" target rates of return could be achieved without illegal conspiratorial meetings. These divisions produce long runs of identical products. Their price tags can be set in the live-and-let-live system of price leadership. The tainted divisions, however, could not enjoy any such stability because most of their products were custom-built. A price quoted for one sale could not be repeated because each sale was unique.

As Professor Robert Lekachman commented, "One need not be derisive in perceiving the complicated collusive arrangements of the electrical equipment cases as apparently sensible extensions of accustomed patterns of behavior. Indeed, there is something strange about condemning some devices which limit competition, among them collusive bidding, and sanctioning others which serve the same purpose, among them price leadership . . ."

Whether or not there were pressures on the executives to conspire, the question of responsibility remains unsettled. Men, after all, are not produced on an assembly line and they don't make identical responses to the same pressure. Outside the corporation, the problem of accountability has been briskly argued. One important view was that of the federal judge who received the indictments, examined much of the evidence and sentenced the defendants. Judge J. Cullen Ganey flatly rejected the thesis that GE and its top management could escape responsibility. He said:

[I am] not at all unmindful that the real blame is to be laid at the doorstep of the corporate defendants and those who guide and direct their policy. While the Department of Justice has acknowledged that they were unable to uncover probative evidence which could secure a conviction beyond a reasonable doubt of those in the highest echelons of the corporations here involved, in a broader sense they bear a grave responsibility for the present situation, for one would be most naive indeed to believe that these violations of the law, so long persisted in, affecting so large a segment of the industry and finally,

involving so many millions upon millions of dollars, were
facts unknown to those responsible for the conduct of the
corporation . . . [I am] convinced that in the greatest number
of these defendants' cases, they were torn between conscience
and an approved corporate policy, with the rewarding objectives of promotion, comfortable security and large salaries—in
short the organization or the company man, the conformist,
who goes along with his superiors and finds balm for his conscience in additional comforts and the security of his place in
the corporate set-up.

Ganey, in effect, turned the doctrine of responsible corporate leaders back on itself. If the new rationale declares that
corporation executives are responsible, then they must take
responsibility for the actions of the institutions they control.
Indeed, Ganey goes further and declares that the top managers had to know and tacitly approve of the illicit acts performed in the tiers beneath them.

However, spokesmen for the two leading business organizations refused to accept Ganey's view, and at least in public
supported Cordiner. John W. McGovern, the president of the
NAM, told an inquiring newspaper, "In a large organization,
you can't know every detail. Things like that could happen
but people at the top would not be aware of it." The president of the Chamber of Commerce, Arthur H. Motley, observed: "As business gets bigger and more decentralized, a
code is written and top management expects everybody to
operate with it. But it must be followed through personally.
It's possible to establish a policy that's not followed."

This confronts the rationale with a peculiar dilemma. Are
corporate leaders responsible when things go well but not
accountable when they don't because the large corporation is
too complex? The Cordiner-McGovern-Motley thesis raises a
cruel suspicion. Is the managerial creed merely an invention
of public relations men to shield large corporations from new

institutional arrangements that would limit their power and insure responsibility?

This dilemma apparently troubled Henry Ford II, chairman of the Ford Motor Co. and a director of GE. Two months after the electrical companies were sentenced Ford delivered a speech on "Business Ethics in 1961."

Noting what he called recent "falls from grace" in the electrical and other industries, Ford declared, ". . . it is the job of our corporate executives to keep their own houses in order."

"I'm afraid it is little use," he said, "to drag out the old bad-apple alibi to explain away things—the idea that there are always a few bad ones in every barrel.

"There is really only one thing for top executives to do at such a time as this. That is to forget the alibis and the explanations and have the fortitude—the plain guts—to stand up and say: 'This is our failure. We are chagrined and sorry. It will not happen again.' "

The speech was widely interpreted as a direct attack on the Vinson-Paxton-Cordiner thesis. Delivered just one week before GE's annual meeting at Syracuse, it appeared to be a hint that Ford and other GE directors would shake up the company's top management. However, at Syracuse, Ford and other outside directors gave Cordiner a vote of confidence, continuing him in his newly enlarged role of both chairman and president.

Some of the most important business institutions in the nation were represented among those GE directors. The board included Charles D. Dickey, a director and member of the executive committee of the Morgan Guaranty Trust Co.; Gilbert W. Humphrey, president of the M. A. Hanna Co., Henry S. Morgan, a partner in Morgan, Stanley & Co., Robert W. Woodruff, chairman of the finance committee, Coca-Cola Co.; Thomas B. McCabe, president of the Scott Paper

Co. and former chairman of the Federal Reserve Board; Donald K. David, vice chairman of the Ford Foundation and former dean of the Harvard Business School; Robert T. Stevens, president of J. P. Stevens & Co. and former Secretary of the Army; and Neil McElroy, chairman of Procter and Gamble Co. and former Secretary of Defense.*

In other words, some of the ranking hierarchs in the business world publicly absolved GE and its top management of responsibility for the conspiracies.

The GE episode illustrates the difficulty of fixing responsibility. Henry Ford's own company afforded a prime example, at about the same time, of the problem of determining just what is responsible conduct.

In his speech on ethics, Ford had confidently asserted, "Business today understands well how its actions may impinge not only on the lives of individuals but also upon the goals and policies of our nation both at home and abroad."

Ford, it can be assumed, was speaking from the heart, for his company had played a conspicuous role in the last great Atlantic trauma of the Eisenhower administration. However, if Ford was also implying that business understanding leads to responsible decisions, Eisenhower himself might have disputed the proposition. To see why, we must go back to the curious gold crisis of October, 1960.

Near the end of the Presidential campaign, a feverish speculative rash broke out in the London market where gold is traded by individuals, banks and even governments. Since the American Treasury stands ready to sell gold to foreign central banks for $35 an ounce, the price of gold in London generally fluctuates near this level. However, in the week of the gold rush, the speculators drove the price up at a dizzy rate. Gold first began climbing in surprising bursts of seven

* McElroy and Woodruff were absent from the Syracuse meeting, but neither have disclosed any dissent from its outcome.

and eight cents an ounce. On October 20, the speculators began running from dollars as if they were infected; the price of gold shot above $40 an ounce. Clearly, the buyers demanding gold at this price were betting that the United States would be forced to devalue the dollar, to change its official price and offer more dollars for gold.

The very act of speculation tended to bring pressure on the United States to devalue. As the gold price mounted, foreign central banks would become increasingly uneasy about holding on to the dollars they had. These banks would be tempted to sell their dollars and demand gold from the shrinking United States supply.

At last, the pressure was relieved. The American Treasury flatly declared that there would be no devaluation and this burst the bubble. By the end of October, the London gold rush was over and the price was sinking back to the official rate. The incident, however, left some questions in bankers' minds. How stable was the dollar? For how long was the Treasury pledge good? After all, governments always promise not to devalue on the very eve of a devaluation.

Behind the belief that the United States would devalue and increase the price it pays for gold was the American deficit in the balance of international payments. However small the deficit may be compared to the nation's total output, whatever the causes responsible for it, a belief in devaluation was not wholly illogical as long as the deficit was increasing. As the earlier discussion related, the deficit means that dollars are accumulating abroad. Under existing monetary arrangements, foreigners send back to the United States a good share of these dollars and demand gold. Since the supply of American gold is limited, one way to stretch it is by an official declaration that each dollar will buy less gold. This is another way of saying "devaluation."

On November 1, President Eisenhower and his Treasury

Secretary, Robert B. Anderson, took to national television to tell the nation that the situation was perilous. "All Americans ought to be profoundly concerned," Anderson intoned.

Perhaps Anderson panicked because he feared that a reckless Democrat was about to be elected President. But two weeks later, Eisenhower acted as if he regarded the fears as genuine. The President, now a lame duck, moved decisively to stem the outflow of dollars and gold. He ordered the Defense Department to reduce by 15,000 a month the number of servicemen's wives and children overseas. He instructed the military in particular and other government agencies in general to slash their dollar spending abroad. And he ordered aid-giving agencies to require their foreign clients to spend almost all the dollars they got on goods and services in the United States.

The President told reporters, "No one likes to break up families but when you are sending out gold dollars all the time —that's what they are now under the present situation—why we have to set a limit."

Estimates of the dollar savings from the Eisenhower orders ranged from $300 million in the first year to an eventual saving of $1 billion a year. The President even hinted that the United States might have to trim its military expenditures in the North Atlantic Treaty Organization to staunch the outflow.

A few day later, the President sent Anderson and the then Under Secretary of State, C. Douglas Dillon, on a humiliating mission to a defeated former enemy. Anderson and Dillon asked the West German government to relieve the strain on the United States balance of payments by assuming some of the bills for American troops in Germany. The Germans, too cunning to make concessions to an outgoing administration, refused.

In the midst of these alarums and excursions, the Ford

company announced it was about to add 360 million of its own dollars to the unfavorable balance of payments.

The sum would be used to buy up the publicly held shares in Ford's British manufacturing subsidiary. The Detroit parent already owned 54.6 percent of Ford Motor Co. of Britain, enough to insure total mastery over every move of the English plant. Nevertheless, Detroit insisted that it needed the remaining 45.4 percent. The announcement was made on November 14, two days before Eisenhower's order recalling military families.

Ford would need British pounds to buy the shares; to get pounds, it would have to pay out dollars. However, the approximately $360 million required would put no strain on Ford of Detroit. The company's cash and marketable securities had leaped to $666.3 million at the end of 1959, a gain of more than $200 million over 1958. Excess cash and near-cash was burning holes in Ford's pockets.

The firm's public statements did not make clear why Ford needed the remaining shares in a company it completely controlled already. Chairman Henry Ford said, "Our major objective in proposing to acquire the minority shares of Ford of England is to obtain greater operational flexibility and to coordinate better our American and European operations so that the Ford group may be able to compete more effectively in world markets. Successful completion of the proposed transaction would permit full coordination of the operations of the English company with those of the American company."

"Coordination" and "flexibility" are fuzzy, bureaucratic words at best. Just how they could become "fuller" or "greater" when Detroit owned 100 percent instead of 55 percent is a still unanswered question.

If the reasoning was muddy, the effect on the conceivably unstable dollar was crystal clear. Ford's decision would send overseas $360 million more of those gold dollars Eisenhower was worried about, possibly more than the entire first year savings from his new austerity program.

A better notion of Ford's motive might be gleaned by examining the high octane performance of the English company. It was simply much more profitable than Ford's Detroit operation. The British plant had been earning nearly 40 percent more on its assets than the corporation as a whole. From 1950 to 1960, Ford sales of cars and trucks built in the United States had climbed only 10 percent; sales of British Ford had risen 15 times as fast.

In other words, the situation appeared to be this: Ford of Detroit had a lot of extra cash lying in the company till; Ford of Britain was a highly profitable operation. So, Ford of Detroit puts its idle cash into the higher yielding shares of its British subsidiary. Ford of Detroit merely acted like an old-fashioned classical entrepreneur, searching for the greatest profits.

Back in Washington, Treasury Secretary Anderson, who had been warning the nation of the dollar's parlous state, got wind of Ford's plans before they were announced. In several phone calls to Chairman Henry, Anderson urged Ford's chief to arrange his deal in such a way as to soften the blow to the balance of payments.* But Ford, presumably with polite regrets, was no kinder to lame ducks than the West Germans. So Ford's dollars flowed out and took some gold with them. In the week that the company sent its check to London for the shares, the United States stock of gold dropped another $204 million.

Ford's behavior would raise no question in a world of atomistic competitors. But in a world of industrial concentra-

---

* The failure of Anderson and Eisenhower to take their request to the public and so enlist public support bespeaks their remarkable ideological devotion to the principle of free capital movement.

tion, Ford's action and timing made a curious contrast with its chairman's claims. Not long before, Ford's general counsel, William T. Gossett, had declared that the measure of the modern corporation's effectiveness in public affairs "is the degree to which its policy reflects the values, objectives, aspirations and reservations of society as a whole."

Whatever Ford was doing in Britain, it had clearly failed to reflect the objectives, aspirations and reservations of a distressed outgoing government.

In their essay on *The Permanent Revolution*, the *Fortune* editors had singled out Ford as an example of the new, responsible corporation. They said: "The Ford company, for example, behaves not as an organization solely dedicated to earning the maximum number of dollars for the Ford family, but as an organization dedicated first of all to its own perpetuation and growth."

To be sure, this was published ten years before Ford opened its own tap on the gold flow.

One more case, involving a folk hero of American business, will illuminate the difficulties surrounding the self-determination of responsible conduct. This is the remarkably unspectacular affair of George Romney's pay from the American Motors Corp. Romney's contribution to AMC and even to society at large is deservedly recognized. He took a dying company and, in a few years, turned it into an unusually healthy specimen. More striking, he demonstrated the value of even limited competition, inducing the major auto producers to turn out functional units of transportation as well as glorified vehicular status symbols. Romney is a devout Mormon of unquestioned piety. His exemplary career has put him in the governor's mansion in Michigan and given him reason to hope for even higher office. Yet Romney, like other well-placed executives, has shown considerable confusion about what constitutes an appropriate financial reward. This confusion stems from a change in the 1950 tax code which gave corporate executives sweeping opportunities to become rich in a hurry.

The restricted stock option, the fashion in most corporations, has provided top officers with a riskless and costless "investment." It has worked in this fashion: Chairman Jones of Deductalot Inc. set up a plan to give himself and other key executives an option or choice to buy shares in the company at a fixed price for as long as ten years. Let us assume that Deductalot's shares were selling at $10.50 each. Jones awarded himself an option to buy 40,000 shares at $10. (He customarily sought approval from his board of directors and the stockholders, but in the complaisant corporate world, this was virtually assured.) If Deductalot's shares dropped in price, he did not buy anything; indeed, he could have reissued the option to buy the shares at a lower price. Let us assume, however, that thanks to his own acumen as a manager or the speculative vagaries of the stock market or for any reason, Deductalot's shares went to $60. Jones then borrowed from the bank the $400,000 he needed to exercise his option, to buy the 40,000 shares at a price of $10. He later sold these shares at $60 and picked up a profit of $2 million.

If he let two years elapse between the original option grant and the sale of his shares, and if he waited at least six months before he sold the shares he bought, he would have been taxed at the capital gains rate. That is, he paid the government no more than 25 percent of his profit or $500,000. This was the same rate paid by a man whose taxable salary income was about $9000. Jones came away with $1.5 million after taxes. The process is riskless because Jones bought only if Deductalot's shares rose. It was costless—apart from some interest payment—if he financed his purchase through a bank loan. Because of stock options, the nation now has a new class of "instant millionaires."

A quiet debate has been staged over the propriety of taxing these gains at only 25 percent instead of the ordinary income tax rate which has been as high as 91 percent. One of the reforms proposed by President Kennedy in 1963 would end the privilege. Proponents generally argue that options tie management's interests to those of shareholders, make managers' rewards dependent on the company's success and induce able managers to join small or risky concerns.

Opponents argue that all these benefits would still be forthcoming if managers were paid in part with company stock or in part with cash bonuses that fluctuated with company profits. The tax privilege, it is contended, is an unnecessary frosting on the executive cake. It induces managers to watch stock ticker tapes more closely than corporate affairs and ties their business decisions to possible stock market consequences rather than some other standard. Finally, the privilege is said to create resentment on the part of other taxpayers who may believe that the revenue system discriminates in favor of corporate managers, the best-paid elite in American society.

AMC set up its first stock option plan in 1954. Romney was allowed to buy 35,000 shares at $9.56 each. In time, as AMC divided its shares and issued dividends in stock, Romney's option grew to embrace 112,455 shares at a cost of $2.98 each. At the end of 1962, AMC was selling at around $16. Thus, if Romney had exercised his options and then sold the shares at the end of 1962, his profit would have exceeded $1.4 million. The government would have taken away 25 percent in taxes and left the AMC chairman with something more than one million dollars.

In fact, Romney began turning the options into cash two years earlier. He borrowed enough to buy 10,000 shares at the original option price of $9.56. He sold them at $90, near AMC's high-water mark. Thus, without putting up money of his own, he made a profit of $800,000. After the tax collector's bite, he was left with $600,000, to say nothing of more

chances at this riskless mint through the exercise of his remaining options.

Again, it must be emphasized that there was nothing unusual in Romney's conduct. It had become standard corporate
behavior. And of course, the option grab bag was placed on
top of the large salaries, generous expense accounts, and handsome performance bonuses that also make up the typical
executive's pay.

For the twelve months before he picked up his option profit
of $600,000, Romney was due to get from AMC $150,000 in
salary and $175,350 in bonuses. This, of course, would be
taxed at ordinary income rates. Romney, who has expressed
his concern over moral issues as frequently and fervently as
any executive, indicated by his words and actions that he was
puzzled over the proper course to take. So he made some
unusual choices. He refused to accept $100,000 of his bonus.
That left him with just $225,350 to be taxed at the regular
income rates. Then, on top of this, there was the $900,000
from the sale of his optioned shares. Romney announced that
he had given as a tithe to his church the handsome sum of
$70,000. From the remaining $830,000, he explained, he had
to subtract two payments of $200,000 each. One went to the
tax collector. The other went to his bank to pay off the
$95,600 he had borrowed to buy the 10,000 shares and to
finance the purchase of some of his remaining options.

"I had to borrow to pick up those options," Romney told
a press conference. "A fellow in my position under the tax
laws is not in a position to buy stock except by borrowing."

Romney seemed to be saying that he got so much ordinary
income that he paid high taxes. And this in turn entitled him
to a riskless, costless "investment" taxed at a bargain rate.
This logic, well understood in executive suites, is a prime instance of the labyrinthine reasoning of executives who try to
justify their ways to man.

The point of this essay is not to argue that businessmen are greedy, hypocritical or irresponsible. To keep score on such questions would pile up an endless number of points on all sides. Here are circumstances suggesting that a television network contributed to an educational station in return for its pledge to display unentertaining programs; there is an oil giant sponsoring superb theater on television; here is a real estate manipulator returning funds he had borrowed from one of his public corporations to put into one of his private ventures; there, a few years earlier, is the same man helping to draw up a code of ethics for his trade; here are the auto companies refusing to charge all that the traffic would bear after World War II; there is the gray market scramble for cars they inadvertently touched off.

The point is that corporate executives, by training and outlook, are ill equipped to make difficult, unchecked judgments in the murky area of social responsibility. Theodore Levitt, a business consultant and more recently on the faculty of the Harvard Business School, has said that the theory of socially responsible businessmen conjures up "the frightening spectacle of a powerful economic functional group whose future and perception are shaped in a tight materialistic context of money and things but which imposes its narrow ideas about a broad spectrum of unrelated noneconomic subjects on the mass of man and society."

Levitt warns that if the corporations are to determine where right conduct lies, we will create "a monolithic society in which the essentially narrow ethos of the business corporation is malignantly extended over everyone and everything."

Berle, the eloquent champion of the conscience-ridden executive, saw through to some other major difficulties of this thesis. "If corporations are to make industrial plans," he asked, "what are the criteria of these plans?" In a world of perfect competition, this question is irrelevant; the consumer is king and his choices, translated through the market, guide business decisions. But in a world of corporations emancipated in some measure from the market, no such criteria exist.

Moreover, Berle observed, modern corporate managements have "substantially absolute power." Even if agreement could be reached on what is and is not responsible behavior, there is no mechanism to make the corporate hierarchs accountable. There is no process whereby society can recall malignant executives or hold a referendum on crucial corporate decisions. If GE's chief officials disclaim responsibility, society is powerless to contradict them effectively.

In sum, a large body of evidence indicates that the corporate conscience is often submerged. Indeed, we lack standards of responsible executive behavior. And if such standards were developed, we have no means to insure that they would be upheld. If the corporate conscience is an uncertain instrument, what can take its place? How can legitimacy and sanction be restored to economic decision making? We appear to be driven back again to the various devices discussed in earlier chapters to shrink corporate power and compel its sharing with other social groups.

To rebut this notion, however, proponents of things as they are move to another line of defense. Perhaps, these theorists argue, the notion of a conscience is overdone and perhaps the best-willed corporate leaders do demonstrate considerable confusion over where self-interest ends and society's begins. But this is no cause for alarm. Corporate power is far from absolute. The executives must deal with organized labor, organized dealers, big suppliers and large customers. Most of all, they confront a more or less representative government with great power of its own. The interplay of these forces, it is asserted, imposes limits to corporate action that more or less compel responsible behavior. This is the doctrine of countervailing power.

5. The Myth of Countervailing Power

GIVEN A WORLD of large and impersonal economic institutions, there is some comfort in believing that the giants collide and neutralize each other. The theory of balancing or offsetting power helps sustain the democratic creed and nourishes economists who hunger for the equilibrium of the classical world. It lies behind the description of America as a pluralistic society; a vision embraced by many academics, journalists, politicians and those corporate officials who are uncomfortable about their power. Even apart from these uses, the concept of strong offsetting blocs has some tangency to the real world. Moreover, it does recognize that there are large and powerful organizations operating on the American scene.

But the confident assertion that these powerful institutions conflict and thereby cancel each other is more wish than fact. Indeed, the theory strains reality even further. It contends that the stalemate not only protects the public against an abuse of power but even yields many of the dividends promised in the classical world of diffused, atomistic power.

Whatever its shortcomings, the theory of countervailing power is undeniably a cornerstone of conventional wisdom. In its crudest form, it argues that Big Business is offset by Big Labor with Big Government watching both. One complication holds that Big Business is divided between Big Buyers and Big Sellers, that Big Producers are confronted

with Big Purchasers, and that their tug of war somehow re-
dounds to the benefit of all. A representative version of the
simple view is David Lilienthal's worshipful essay on the giant
corporations. He writes:

"In short, as a result of the new comprehensive role of
Government in economic affairs, the new power and influence
of organized labor, the rise of the New Competition . . . a
change in the power of large buyers . . . a change as to the
social responsibility of Big Business . . . corporate control
. . . is now divided and diffused . . . Against the danger of
Bigness . . . we either already have adequate public safeguards, or know how to fashion new ones as required."

A more sophisticated elaboration is Professor Galbraith's
witty and urbane treatise, *American Capitalism: The Concept
of Countervailing Power*. Galbraith offers so many fruitful
insights into the economic order that his book and his ter-
minology have enjoyed a well-deserved vogue. Stripped of
important qualifications and exceptions, Galbraith's central
thesis is that the power of corporation managers, "though
considerable, is deployed against others who are strong enough
to resist any harmful exercise of such power." As a prescription for what should be, this notion may be unimpeachable.
But as a description of what is, it is less than adequate.

One of Galbraith's most ingenious contributions is his conclusion that strong sellers beget strong buyers. This idea is so
crucial to the theory that it deserves a closer look. At the
retail level, Galbraith contends, these strong buyers exercise
their countervailing power on behalf of consumers. Thus, in
his view, the great chains like A & P, the great mail order
houses like Sears, Roebuck and the great department stores
like Macy's force concessions from the concentrated producers
of goods and thereby give lower prices to consumers.

Galbraith's thesis begins to crumble at earlier stages in the
productive process. Here, it is not likely that consumers derive

much benefit from the big buyers. Think of American Telephone and Telegraph subsidiaries buying Anaconda's copper, of General Motors' purchases from U.S. Steel, of Consolidated Edison buying generators from General Electric.

There is no reason why these giant customers, partly or entirely free from competitive pressures, should force great concessions from their giant suppliers. At the production level, they operate in a live-and-let-live milieu. Why should they behave any differently when they are buyers? Even if the big buyers should extract concessions, what force compels them to be passed on to the dealers or consumers? In its quest for target returns, the corporate world wants stable prices and settles for higher prices as a second best. Price cutting is the last refuge to which corporation executives want to be driven. This fear of lower prices is reinforced by the prevailing corporate belief that demand is largely inelastic. That is, the typical corporation believes it won't gain enough extra sales from lower prices to compensate for the reduced revenue on each unit of sale. Given this frame of mind, corporations lack strong incentives to bargain down and pass on to consumers lower costs of supplies. Certainly the regulated telephone and electric utilities have little incentive to shop for lower costs. Their charges are set to yield a more or less fixed rate of return. The utilities are prevented in effect from pocketing any cost savings. And on the other side of that coin, increased copper or machinery costs can be translated into higher rates for consumers with the blessings of the regulatory commission.

In some industries, buyers and sellers are under the same corporate roof and obviously no genuine tug of war will take place. Crude oil production and refining afford a striking illustration of an industry in which some giants combine instead of countervail. In the Texas fields, the biggest buyers reporting their demand to the state regulatory agency in any month are subsidiaries of Standard Oil Co. (New Jersey),

Standard Oil Co. (California), Standard Oil Co. (Indiana) and other giant producers.

In sum, whenever the big buyers are also big producers in a concentrated industry or whenever big buyers and big sellers are different arms of the same corporation, there are no grounds for believing that the ultimate consumer will enjoy any particular benefits from their dealings. If consumers are to gain from a struggle between buyers and sellers, the buyers who sell to consumers must be under strong competitive pressures.

Galbraith's selection of retailing to illustrate the theory of beneficient countervails is strategic. Despite the growth of chains linking many small stores or even large department stores, there is plenty of competition and relatively less concentration in this sector of the economy.

The trouble, as Professor George Stigler has observed, is that these large selling units buy most of their products from unconcentrated industries. Even if the chains are hard bargainers and share the fruits of their bargaining with consumers, they are buying from more or less weak sellers. The mail order chains and big department stores sell furniture and clothing chiefly; neither industry is dominated by a Big Four or Big Five. The A & P, Safeway and other grocery chains sell food; but farmers provide the textbook example of classical competitive markets. (Galbraith might retort with considerable justification that the Government has come to the aid of the farmers, giving them countervailing power in the form of price supports. While this may help shore up farm income, it is far from clear how it lowers prices to consumers.)

The other goods that consumers buy are generally distributed by weak sellers. These markets are characterized by a few giants on one side, the producing side, and a regiment of pigmies on the other, the retail side. The relative handful who manufacture autos, refine gasoline, make cigarettes, pour steel or manufacture building materials distribute through dealers or retailers who are rarely little more than dependent captives of the producers themselves. The local gas station, candy store or even Chevrolet dealer is not likely to impress Standard Oil Co. (New Jersey), The American Tobacco Co. or General Motors with his countervailing power.

Galbraith himself acknowledged that the beneficent potential of his countervailing model would be frustrated in inflation. When demand is strong, he remarked, the big buyers won't haggle with the big sellers but will simply pass on higher costs to consumers. Writing in 1956, Galbraith could hardly discuss the peculiar sluggishness and absence of inflation that has marked the economy since 1958. Under these conditions, it appears that big buyers won't press big sellers very hard, either. The big buyers may be less willing than they are in headier, inflationary times to pass on sellers' price increases. But there is no sign that the large buyers have been strenuously attempting to push prices down or even resisting modest increases by their suppliers.

At one point in his essay, Galbraith declared that some unemployment of men and plants is "an absolute and inescapable requirement for [price] stability in industries characterized by a generally developed countervailing power. Some slack in the economy is what keeps countervailing power from being converted into a coalition against the public."

This was a prescient forecast of the economy's next turn. But it hardly makes countervailing power, even where it exists, a very appetizing state of affairs. It leaves the public with a choice of inflation or unemployment.

If countervailing power in the corporate world is either nonexistent or malignant, can we hope for more from the confrontation of Big Labor with Big Business? The image of two equal and offsetting giants is particularly appealing to some celebrants of things as they are. Against corporate power, they cite strikes, large and wealthy unions and the prestigious positions of some union leaders. Thus the doctrine of pluralistic power is reaffirmed.

Whatever its value as a social and political check on the power of business, there is plenty of evidence that the confrontation between unions and managers often evolves into accommodation rather than conflict on the economic front. Again, Galbraith perceived this. When demand is strong, he said, "it is to the mutual advantage of union and employer to effect a coalition and to pass the costs of their agreement on in higher prices."

The coalition, of course, need not be overt, need not be collusive. Acting independently, countervails may coalesce and the consumer pays the price. The most striking example is the price-wage spiral that uncoiled in the steel industry from the end of World War II until the economy began to flatten out in 1958. The affair assumed a ritual nature. The United Steelworkers would press for a large wage increase. After some show of reluctance, the industry would grant a big packet and then use the bargain as an excuse to gain more than compensating price increases.*

Twice during periods of government price control, the companies in effect invited the union to strike for higher prices as well as higher pay. In 1946 and 1952, the steel industry refused to accept government-approved wage increases until the government also agreed to enlarge its suggested price increase. Both strikes were successful from the companies' standpoint; both made signal contributions to smashing World War II and Korean War wage and price controls.

A study for the Joint Economic Committee concluded that the rapid rise in postwar steel prices had been due to:

* In the spiral's most virulent period during the 1950's, the union increased its members' pay and fringe benefits enough to lift steelmaking costs by 18 to 19 percent, according to Gardiner Means. But the companies raised prices by 36 percent.

(1) An extraordinary rise in wages which is the result of bargaining between a strong union and a management with strong market power in the product market. Government intervention has probably accelerated this process.

(2) A conscious effort to maintain and perhaps increase profit margins in the industry, giving the steel companies at the least a proportionate share of the income gains scored at the expense of the rest of the economy.

This little game of ring around the price-wage spiral began coming to an end in 1959 when demand in the economy generally was weakening and the public and the government became more aware of its unhappy consequences.

Steel is big and visible. But steel is not unique. Throughout the American economy, unions and managers are sometimes colliding but often combining in a fashion that would confound Karl Marx, Adam Smith and the more optimistic adherents of countervailing power. These combinations probably offend at least as often as they serve the public interest.

A remarkable example can be found in the maritime industry—although admittedly shipping is a grotesque affair, a caricature of American industrial life. In this sector, the two leading unions tend to fight each other and to ally themselves with two separate sets of shipowners. Instead of offsetting the two types of carrier, the unions reinforce them.

One labor organization is the National Maritime Union or NMU. Its men sail for the most part on ships that receive building and operating subsidies from the federal government. The other union is the Seafarers International or SIU. Its membership is concentrated in lines that receive no such handouts.* The NMU works so closely with the major sub-

---

* The inter-union rivalry is often ascribed to the thorny personalities of the two dominant leaders, Joe Curran and Paul Hall. Or it is blamed on their different CIO and AFL parentage. But neither factor is now so important as the differing economic interests of the shipowners with whom they bargain.

sidized lines that they share the expenses of a Washington office for promoting bigger subsidies. The SIU has been looking for a formula that will weld it to its unsubsidized lines in a common effort to get a piece of this pie.

The strain between the two union-employer alliances led to a bizarre situation during the bargaining and strike of 1961. Then, the SIU found itself in the anomalous position of protesting the enormous wage increase that the subsidized lines were granting the NMU. The subsidized lines couldn't have cared less because the taxpayer would foot much of the added cost burden. The SIU's leaders knew they were undermining their position with their own members by asking for smaller gains than the NMU. But the SIU feared even more bankrupting some of its own nonsubsidized lines who would have to pay for the increase out of their own pockets. In the end, government mediators virtually compelled the SIU and its companies to accept the "bargain" struck by the NMU and its subsidized operators.

Scattered throughout the economy are similar union-industry alliances, typically in sectors that lack the price and market controlling influence of a few big firms. The International Ladies Garment Workers stabilizes the atomistic manufacturers of women's apparel. The United Hatters, Cap and Millinery Workers makes loans to keep alive weak (and possibly inefficient) hat companies. The United Mine Workers gives financial aid to large mines, helping to drive smaller, high cost and low paying companies to the wall. The Teamsters Union gives concessions in the terms of its contracts to large truckers and thereby promotes President James Hoffa's aim of eliminating the smaller firms. In some cities, building trades unions and contractors decide together who can bid on what jobs; at the national level, the construction unions and large employers collaborate to prevent industrial concerns from using their own workers on building tasks. On a much smaller scale, the secretary-treasurer of the New York newspaper reporters union in 1962 openly urged publishers during a strike to raise their circulation and advertising rates in order to pay bigger salaries. Whatever this was worth, two New York morning newspapers doubled their price after the strike was settled.

Apart from wages, prices and shares of markets, unions and employers collaborate in other ways that muddy the picture of offsetting power. Unions and management often lobby for joint ends. Thus, the Communications Workers of America supported A T & T's successful struggle for a private satellite communications company; the Amalgamated Clothing Workers led the industry's drive to curb imports of Japanese textiles; and the Mine Workers are the industry's spearhead against imports of residual fuel oil.

This does not mean that unions and management never conflict. They obviously and frequently do. But even in the absence of the strong demand cited by Galbraith, an extraordinary range of parallel and possibly antisocial combination takes place. Moreover, if the economy does emerge from the stagnation that has gripped it in recent years, its renewed strength could be dissipated by tacit combination. In those industries dominated by strong unions and concentrated producers, a revival of the wage-price game played by steel is a distinct possibility. The resulting rise in prices would then eat up part or all of the expanded demand.

Apart from the various forms of combination, the popular notion of offsetting blocs is endangered on another front. The simple fact is that union power has been slowly ebbing away. Despite the noisy outcries over inconvenient strikes, Big Labor can't be equated with Big Business by capitalizing four words. The well-publicized union treasuries, the gleaming Washington headquarters and the infrequent, lengthy shutdowns give a misleading picture of union power. By the early

1960's, unions as a whole were losing about as many members as they were enrolling; their prospects of merely keeping pace with the growth of the labor force were dim. In the words of Sidney Lens, the typical union had become "an institution which carries out its accepted tasks in routine fashion, by rote, rather than . . . missionary force."

Behind this condition is the changing nature of the American economy and the comfortable, twilight repose of an entrenched leadership. The new economy is expanding in the very sectors where unions are weak or nonexistent and shrinking in the strongholds of unionism. In traditional union bastions like railroads and coal mining, jobs are vanishing under the impact of competing modes of transportation and fuel and a new technology that replaces men with machines. Between 1947 and 1961, two-thirds of the bituminous coal mining jobs disappeared; in railroads, about two of five. In the primary metals industries—steel, copper and aluminum—more than one production job in six had vanished. The sectors of growing employment are finance, real estate, retailing and government. Here, union organization has generally been weak. At the AFL–CIO's 1961 convention, the federation's director of organization, John Livingston, lamented that unions had enrolled less than 15 percent of the 8 million service trades workers, the 6.5 million retail and wholesale workers and the 9 million on local, state and federal payrolls. Optimists might point to a sharp rise in the membership of two government unions. They had expanded from 150,000 to nearly 260,000 between 1955 and 1961. But this was still a small fraction of the potential membership. The only major sector where unions are strong and employment is expected to rise rapidly is the construction industry.

The transformation of industrial sectors has been accompanied by a shift in occupations and the consequences for the unions are just as dismal. In the new automated, service-using economy, the nature of work is changing rapidly, and the unions are losing out. White collar clerks, technicians and professionals are growing; the blue collar semi-skilled worker, heart of the union, is falling back. For the first time in 1956, the number of white collar workers exceeded the number of blue collars. By 1962, 29.9 million workers wore white collars compared to 20.2 million in 1947. This increase accounted for nearly all of the gain in jobs during the fifteen year period. Even within union citadels in the mass production industries, the largely nonunion professional, clerical, sales and technical forces are gaining ground on the workers at assembly lines. In 1947, there were seven production workers for each nonproduction worker in primary metals. Fifteen years later, there were only four. Similarly in the transportation equipment industry, autos and aircraft, the number of white collars had risen from a little more than one in six to nearly one in three. Almost every union convention deplores labor's inability to organize the white collar workers; labor strategists meet from time to time to design campaigns for the capture of these groups. But despite a flood of paper and words, the unions have made little progress in this enlarging sphere and show little sign of doing better.

Finally, an important postwar shift has taken place in industry's geographical location. The fastest growing regions of employment are the South and the West, historically indifferent or hostile to unions; jobs in the friendlier climate of the Northeast are also increasing but at a much slower rate. From 1947 to 1962, the number of nonfarm jobs in New England, the Middle Atlantic and the East North Central states rose less than 15 percent. But the number in the South Atlantic states climbed more than 40 percent, in the Mountain States, 70 percent and on the Pacific Coast more than 60 percent. Moreover, the new plants in any region tend to be built outside of cities, where unions are strong. Instead, they spring up in the suburbs or rural areas where the local community and its government are at best cool towards organized labor.

These shifts within and between industries, in the nature of work and the location of industry have not reduced total union membership. But labor's rolls have generally remained static while the number of jobs slowly advances. The AFL–CIO estimated that labor had organized about 40 percent of its potential in 1953; by 1961, this had fallen to 38 percent. A union's power, like a corporation's, depends on its ability to impose its will. At the economic level, this power ultimately hinges on the union's ability to halt a productive process. In many sectors, unions still possess this strength; but in many of the rising sectors of the economy, this power is negligible or nonexistent.*

Moreover, even in those areas where a union's numerical strength is still great, its ability to exercise power has been undermined by the changed climate of opinion created since the end of the war. The real gains in material well-being for many union members and the widely publicized greed and thievery of some labor leaders have weakened public sympathy for unions and alienated many of labor's strategic intellectual and liberal supporters. "The image of the union as the social conscience of the community has been considerably dimmed,"

* One of the most common fallacies holds that "Jimmy Hoffa can stop the nation's wheels." Some arithmetic shows how little there is in this. Hoffa's membership includes at a generous estimate about 1.3 million truck drivers or enough to man perhaps 700,000 trucks. In 1961, there were 12.3 million trucks registered in the United States, or 17 for every one in Hoffa's domain. Hoffa's union embraces largely common carrier or for-hire trucks. But a large share of truck traffic moves on private fleets, outside the Teamsters' sway. Moreover, freight also moves on rails, barges, pipelines, ships and planes. In 1961 trucks accounted for less than one of every four freight ton-miles in intercity traffic. In other words, Hoffa at best "controls" a small fraction of trucking and trucks carry only a portion of all the freight. Hoffa could, if he dared, play hob with some particular city's food supply, but it is patent nonsense to talk of his halting the nation's transport.

observes Solomon Barkin, former research director of the Textile Workers Union.

The new climate encouraged the passage of two important, constricting laws, the Taft-Hartley and Landrum-Griffin Acts. They have encouraged few defections from existing unions but they have raised barriers against organizing the unorganized. In a society heavily conditioned by business values, unions have always been disadvantaged; in the postwar world, these disadvantages have multiplied, partly because of union success and partly because of union excess. Despite the speeches proclaiming that unions have arrived and are accepted, the view of C. Wright Mills seems much more accurate. "The union, unlike the corporation," he said, "is often in a state of protest; it is on the defensive in a sometimes actually, and always potentially, hostile society."

Finally, for all its current strains and failings, the war and postwar economy has brought an increase in well-being for many groups in the population. The widespread social discontent of the 1930's has evaporated. Today's deprived racial minorities and the largely inarticulate poverty-ridden white minority are forces of a different and smaller magnitude. As instruments of protest, unions in this new setting are less successful in mobilizing their members or embracing new groups of unorganized workers.

So far, this account has focused on the external reasons for labor's shrinking power. But this is not the whole story. Within labor's house, some of the beams are rotten and others are petrified. Working in comfortable executive suites, riding in union-financed limousines and commanding small bureaucratic armies, labor's leaders generally are complacent. Down the line, organizers and other functionaries either reflect or can't overcome this self-satisfaction. The missionary zeal that marked the organizing upsurge of the 1930's is gone.

"A certain lassitude has overtaken the trade union movement itself. Little is left of the proselytizing spirit," Barkin writes. Dave Beck's union-paid silk undershirts from Sulka are a flamboyant symbol of the new, higher life. But even the majority of honest union leaders live in a different world from the rank and file. They are amused by or scornful of the comparatively ascetic Walter Reuther who receives $24,040 a year in salary but won't use his expense account for a tax-free joyride through the padded life.*

Comfort and complacency are dull spurs for organizing. Many unions don't want to risk their treasuries and other assets in dubious ventures. Even within their own historic jurisdictions, they don't want to be bothered. In some cities, the powerful building tradesmen are reluctant to move into the heavily nonunionized home building field; this would mean opening their rolls to new members who might someday compete for jobs or upset an established leadership. When Reuther makes fiery speeches about the need to mount organizing campaigns, Meany asks him why he has failed to bring the auto industry's growing white collar army under the United Auto Workers' banner.

Instead of competing to organize the unorganized as unions often did in the 1930's, much of today's competition is a kind of piracy. Unions hunt each other's members or try to carve out control over the work performed by another union. Fi-

---

* The current style was underscored by an exchange at the 1961 AFL–CIO convention. President Michael Quill of the Transport Workers Union, who likes to pose in the militant stance he regularly assumed a generation ago, taunted the delegates assembled in the plush Miami Beach hotel by declaring: "This convention should be held in Montgomery, Alabama as a challenge to the White Citizens Council and the John Birch Society. Oh, I grant you we won't have so many swimming pools. I grant you the massage room would not be so busy, because the only people who do the massaging down there are the people with the sheriff's clubs and the police who bend them over the heads of the workers." President George Meany of the AFL–CIO lamely replied: "Hearing him brought back some fond memories when Mike and I used to meet once a week in the massage room of the Hotel Astor, where we discussed Mike's arthritis and my inability to keep my weight down."

nally, the AFL–CIO's cautious treatment of craft unions that bar Negro members has further compromised labor's missionary claims.

In mature unions, Professor Richard Lester concludes, the leaders "are organization men" and their institutions act like "sleepy monopolies." Short of imagination and fresh ideas, lacking the broader social vision that might attract the rising white collar and technical workers, organized labor contributes heavily to its own frustrations.

If labor's economic power has been vastly overrated, its political strength has also been magnified out of all proportion. At the national level, labor's leaders have drifted into a satellite role within the Democratic Party. Union political endorsements are nearly as predictable as the movement of the planets. At the local levels, too, most union officials have become an integral part of a city or state machine, usually Democratic but occasionally Republican. The rewards for this loyalty have been largely honorific; prestige and place, positions on boards and commissions, an occasional ambassadorship, a few assistant secretaryships when the Democrats control the White House. The unions, in short, have fallen into what Mills called a nest of "status traps." But the price for this has been a marginal influence on programs and policies. A hard core of Representatives and even fewer Senators are wholly responsive to labor's organized views; they constitute a distinct minority.

Within the Democratic Party, union leaders enjoy some negative power. If they unite at state and national conventions, they can usually veto an unacceptable candidate. Except perhaps in Michigan, however, they are rarely able by themselves to select a ticket.

On the other hand, union members provide their organizations with more potential political strength than popular accounts suggest. The rank and file tend to follow the voting recommendations of their leaders with considerable fidelity. *When Labor Votes*, an intensive study of this question, looked at Detroit auto workers and concluded that most trust their union's endorsements and that "the great majority cast their ballots accordingly." But despite the loyalty of the rank and file on election day, the unions have become so much a part of existing political machinery that they can be and are taken for granted when policy and program decisions are made.

A striking example of just this occurred in the summer of 1962. The AFL–CIO was then as it had been for several years on record as favoring an immediate tax cut. But when the House Ways and Means Committee began hearings on a possible emergency reduction, Meany and other federation hierarchs were uncertain about their course. Some of Meany's staff strongly urged him not to endorse tax reduction because President Kennedy might not publicly favor it at that time. Others argued that Meany could not reject labor's own established position. Meany settled his dilemma by personally asking Kennedy what to do. The President told Meany that he should adhere to labor's line and so, with Kennedy's approval, Meany reaffirmed the AFL–CIO stand.

If labor's president has to ask the leader of the Democratic Party what position to take on a central issue of labor concern, and one on which the federation had already spoken, union legislative proposals are not likely to be regarded as imperatives by politicians of any stripe.

"Trade unions are essential to an effective decentralized, pluralistic democratic society," Barkin says. "If they are weakened, the base for this society is itself weakened."

Labor's power is, even in an automating society, of great potential magnitude. Sometimes this power is displayed (and then some pluralizers think they detect excessive strength). But since the end of the second world war, this power has been confined to increasingly less important sectors of economic and political life. The erosion, however, has neither been startling enough nor rapid enough to shake most union leaders and their members from accustomed routines. But the steady decline in union power, coupled with the growing number of areas where unions and employers combine, unravels the concept of Big Labor as a countervailing force.

The artists of the political balancing act, however, have one more pole to swing. If Big Labor is a dubious offset, what about Big Government? Galbraith declared that "the support of countervailing power has become in modern times perhaps the major domestic peacetime function of the federal government." And Lilienthal, it will be recalled, assured his audience that "against the danger of Bigness . . . we either already have adequate public safeguards, or know how to fashion new ones as required."

If Big Government is indeed a countervail to Big Business, then an innocent observer might expect that the performance of the great federal regulatory agencies would support this view. These independent commissions, supposedly insulated from political manipulation, were created to rule over transportation, communications and the distribution of power, among other spheres. Their record, however, gives little comfort to the theorists of balance. Indeed, the overwhelming testimony is that the regulators in time become the captives of the regulated, that the commissions become the creatures of the industries they are supposed to police. This is not simply a question of venality; this is the record of nearly every agency since the establishment of the first in 1887.

As the agencies mature, after the flush of reforming zeal that called them into being has passed, here is what happens according to Professor Marver H. Bernstein of Princeton:

> The approach and point of view of the regulatory process begin to partake of those of business management . . . the commission becomes more concerned with the general health

of the industry and tries to prevent changes which adversely affect it. Cut off from the mainstream of political life, the commission's standards of regulation are determined in the light of the desires of the industry affected. It is unlikely that the commission, in this period, will be able to extend regulation beyond the limits acceptable to the regulated groups . . . The close of the period of maturity is marked by the commission's surrender to the regulated . . . the commission finally becomes a captive of the regulated groups.

From inside the commissions, the same story is told. Here is Louis J. Hector, writing to President Eisenhower after resigning from the Civil Aeronautics Board.

But no man can possibly work all day every day with the same people in the same industry . . . and then from time to time wipe out every bit of that out of his mind in order to become a judge . . . Commissioners circulate more or less freely in the industry they regulate . . . [Later] the same commissioner climbs on the bench and is supposed suddenly to become a judge . . . The system is actually so inviting to improper influence that it will inevitably occur from time to time.

Here is Howard Morgan, writing to President Kennedy as he resigns from the Federal Power Commission:

Abandonment of the public interest can be caused by many things, of which timidity and a desire for personal security are the most insidious, the least detectable and, once established in a regulatory agency, the hardest to eradicate. Without the needed sense of public responsibility, a commissioner can find it very easy to consider whether his vote might arouse an industry campaign against his reconfirmation by the Senate, and even easier to convince himself that no such thought ever crossed his mind.

When commissioners lack character and courage, Morgan said, implying that his peers were deficient in both, "utility regulation ceases to be or never becomes a protection to the consuming public. Instead it can easily become a fraud upon the public and a protective shield behind which monoply may operate to the public detriment."

One of the strongest supporters of the regulatory technique is James M. Landis, a former chairman of the Securities and Exchange Commission. But in a pre-inaugural report to Kennedy, Landis warned the incoming President of a problem. Landis said that agency members become so oriented to the industry they are regulating that they identify the industry's interest and the public interest as one.

This trait is so pronounced that Professor Samuel Huntington has given it a name, "clientalism." In a study of the transportation agencies, he concluded that agency and industry "tend to fuse into one smooth harmonious whole with a common purpose and a common outlook." Huntington continued: "If there is any complaint about the activities of the client-group the cliental agency can always be pointed to in defense as proof that the matter is actually in proper hands."

Legislators of both parties have pronounced in a similar vein. Senator George D. Aiken, Republican of Vermont, observed in 1951: "It takes almost superhuman powers on the part of a regulatory commissioner, after he has been in office for a certain length of time, not to promote the business he is supposed to regulate instead of regulating it."

Senator Paul H. Douglas, Democrat of Illinois, responded: ". . . a man has to be of heroic mold . . . once he gets on the commissions, to be militant in defense of the general interest. Since by definition, the number of heroes is limited, does that not put the public at something of a disadvantage?"

The authorities could be cited without end, but perhaps one more should be invoked. In 1892, Attorney General Richard Olney, a prominent corporation lawyer, wrote a far-sighted and soothing letter to a railroad president who thought that the recently created Interstate Commerce Commission should be destroyed.

> The Commission, as its functions have now been limited by the courts, is or can be made of great use to the railroads. It satisfies the popular clamor for a government supervision of railroads, at the same time that that supervision is almost entirely nominal. Further, the older such a Commission gets to be, the more inclined it will be found to take the business and railroad view of things. It thus becomes a sort of barrier between the railroad corporations and the people and a sort of protection against hasty and crude legislation hostile to railroad interests . . . The part of wisdom is not to destroy the Commission but to utilize it.

Olney's vision was realized beyond his fondest hopes. The ICC has become over the years so much of a tool of the railroads (except for the bureau regulating trucks which is a sturdy defender of trucking interests), that it is almost killing the lines with kindness. The ICC's habit of indiscriminately granting whatever rate increases the carriers seek has helped to drive freight and passengers to other modes of transportation.

The same story of subservience is found in most of the other regulatory agencies. The Federal Power Commission refused for years to enforce a Supreme Court decision requiring the agency to fix the prices charged by independent natural gas producers. In those sectors where the FPC has set prices, Landis observed, the agency has displayed "disregard of the consumer interest." This disregard is so flagrant that state regulatory agencies have had to fight FPC's efforts to impose "monopolistic and excessive rates." That's the rare case of man bites dog. Normally, it is the state commissions who are most easily controlled by client industries and the federal government that offers consumers relatively stronger protection.

Similarly, the Civil Aeronautics Board has zealously protected the major airlines. The CAB shielded them from new competition by strangling with harassing regulations the non-scheduled airlines that flourished after the war and by refusing to certify any new scheduled airline despite the rapid growth in air travel. Again, the Federal Communication Commission's responsiveness to the television and radio networks has been so notorious that President Kennedy tried to give a new character to this servile and corrupted agency by staffing it with some of the most independent of the New Frontiersmen.

Students of the regulatory agencies have quarreled over whether the FPC or the FCC has most faithfully served its industry's narrow interests. There is good reason, however, to award the prize to the little-noticed Federal Maritime Board. After an intensive examination the House Antitrust Subcommittee concluded in 1962 that the Board had been an "almost complete failure" as an effective regulatory force over ocean shipping. Like so many other agencies, its employees regarded the Board "as a way station on the road to private advancement." In the words of the Subcommittee, "The Board's degeneration may also be attributable to the fact that its members and its staff frequently found refuge in the shipping industry upon the expiration of their service with the Board."

By taking a close look at the records of "relatively few lines," the Subcommittee uncovered 240 possible violations of federal laws—illegal kickbacks to customers, illegal rate-fixing agreements and the like—all of them ignored by the agency. The situation was so bad that the Board's regulatory and subsidy-giving functions were divided in a 1961 reorganization and a new Maritime Commission and a new Maritime Administration put in its place.

What is the prognosis for structural reform of this kind? Many of the critics believe that changing a commission's tasks or bringing in new and stronger members can salvage the agencies as instruments of the public interest. Professor Bernstein would make them more responsive to popular political forces; former Commissioner Hector would strip them of their judicial and prosecuting functions; former Commissioner Morgan would, like Diogenes, search for better men. However, history is not on the reformers' side. A variety of agency structures and personalities have, over time, followed a sort of Darwinian law: survival depends on adaptation to the demands of the regulated.

Is life very different in the executive departments, the agencies directly under the Presidential wing? This question has not received anything like the scholarly attention devoted to the regulatory agencies. But some tentative answers can be made.

Students of the regulatory commissions often cite three reasons for the servility of the agencies: commission procedures do not allow a public representative or public counsel to press consumer views, so only an industry voice is heard; the commissioners tend to come from private industry and to leave government for the very industry they had been "regulating"; and, finally, the regulated industries can and do keep up a steady, one-sided pressure on their regulators. But there is nothing about these factors that is unique to the commissions. They are all present with varying degrees of intensity in the executive departments. When the Treasury, for example, plans to float a bond issue, it consults committees of bankers to find out what they want. The Agriculture Department tends to regard itself as the farmers' representative, not as a public interest body. Its subdivisions generally reflect the views of the commodity producers whom the bureaus are promoting as well as regulating.

Perhaps the process can be observed most nakedly in the Interior Department's Bureau of Mines and its treatment of petroleum. Oil production, unlike refining and transportation, is not concentrated but is divided among thousands of big and small concerns. In the name of conservation, the principal oil producing states set production quotas each month, limiting the amount that the wells may bring up. These state quotas, in turn, are based on forecasts made by the Bureau of Mines. The reports calculate the amount of oil that can be sold at existing prices. The system is reinforced by a prohibition against the interstate shipment of oil produced outside of a state quota and by curbs on the quantity of oil that can be imported. Here then is a complex federal-state system designed to keep oil prices above the production costs of relatively inefficient producers by tailoring supply to demand at going prices.

"Concern for the conservation of a scarce and essential raw material was made a justification for regulation, but the real stimulus to regulatory action was the desire of oil producers and allied interests to promote their own economic welfare."

This is the conclusion of a standard text, *Government and the American Economy* by Merle Fainsod, Lincoln Gordon and Joseph C. Palamountain. In other words, the state agencies and the Bureau of Mines become a legal substitute for a Big Three or for an illegal conspiracy to set prices.

In sum, the Big Government of the Cabinet departments suffers many of the defects of the regulatory agencies. The notion that either or both is an effective countervail to corporate power is dubious as long as the departments, bureaus and agencies are organized functionally, created to serve, regulate and promote separate producers and industries. The parochial nature of their task tends to turn officials of even the best will from broad-based public considerations to the establishment of a symbiotic partnership with the industry to which they are engaged. If a mechanism could be created so that government agencies and their client industries, as a matter of self-interest, thought in terms of the whole economy and the whole society, if representatives from other groups in the public were given a voice in their councils, a different result might take place. But in the present state of affairs, the government is much more likely to combine with than to offset business power.

The Cold War has added a new dimension to this problem. One of its principal consequences has been to blur the line between public and private functions. Under the impact of enormous military expenditures, government and private industry have become entangled at an astonishing number of points. The combination is most visible in the flow of top officials who shuttle between high military and government posts to corporate presidencies and directorships. Less apparent but just as important are the new ways in which the government conducts defense business.

The importance of the national security sector in the nation's economy cannot be exaggerated. For the accounting year ending on June 30, 1964, $56 billion was allotted to defense and space tasks, nearly three of every five dollars in the government's conventional budget and about 10 percent of the economy's total output.

Major industries have grown up almost entirely dependent on government military orders; others draw a substantial portion of their income from military buying. The companies in the aerospace industry receive from two-thirds to 99 percent of their total business from military purchases. The leading electrical machinery producers, General Electric and Westinghouse make nearly a third of their sales to defense buyers.

This breeds a dependency that works two ways. Government agencies become as bound to their military suppliers as the military suppliers to their federal customer. So, the Defense Department will deliberately award orders to a less efficient producer to maintain that producer's productive capacity. Officials in charge of the government's stockpile of strategic materials testified they had bought more than they needed to support the prices and profits of their industrial suppliers. A military service or its bureaus will develop as much of a vested interest in one company's weapon design as the company itself. The prestige and power of the service will depend on the appropriations it gets and this in turn may hinge on the approval of its chosen company's design. Just as some trade unions have fought against ending production of an obsolete weapon in order to preserve members' jobs, so too service officers struggle to hold what they have and to expand their domain.

The line between private and public becomes fuzziest, however, in the new administrative arrangements for parceling out defense business. The government does not as a rule award contracts for a rocket engine, a firing mechanism or the construction of a launching site. Instead, it hires a firm to produce a "weapons system" complete from soup to nuts, from blueprints to installation and possibly even operation. Indeed, the firm holding the prime or original contract for such a system will probably draw up the menu itself. The military agency may merely describe what characteristics a new weapon should have and let the prime contractor invent one to fit. The design and production of component parts and the erection of facilities like launching sites will be distributed by this prime contractor downward through successive tiers of subcontractors.

Since no one can reasonably estimate the cost of something that is yet to be invented, the military does not usually award these contracts by competitive bids to the lowest cost firm. Instead, the Defense Department typically negotiates with one firm, or a few selected firms, promising to cover all costs and add on a fixed fee for profit.

In this new twilight world, the government has turned over an endless variety of functions to private groups. Dean Don K. Price of the School of Public Administration at Harvard has noted "that private corporations have contracts to maintain the Air Force's bombers and its missile ranges, private institutions make strategic studies for the Joint Chiefs of Staff and foreign policy studies for the Senate Foreign Relations Committee, universities administer technical-assistance programs for the State Department all over the world, and telephone and radio companies are about to help the National Aeronautics and Space Administration carry our messages through outer space."

One study of the new defense contracting concludes: "While private firms have thus been freed from the restraints of the open market, they have acquired new public responsibilities. They are no longer merely suppliers to the government, but participants in the administration of public functions."

In this new world, arms length bargaining between independent parties disappears. Instead, as E. Perkins McGuire, former Assistant Secretary of Defense, said: "Some of these contractors by the very magnitude of the procurement we are involved in *are in reality agents of the government.*"

The two quotations underline the ambiguity of the new relationship. One suggests that the private firms have become public administrators; the other, that they are really government instruments. In either case, it is clear that they are not simply selling goods and services to a public customer.

The eggs have been so thoroughly scrambled that government officials are becoming worried about a silent abdication of responsibility. In a report to President Kennedy, some of his top advisers generally applauded the new partnership in contracting for research and development. However, the report, signed by Defense Secretary Robert S. McNamara among others, acknowledged "that in recent years there have been instances—particularly in the Department of Defense—

where we have come dangerously close to permitting contract employees to exercise functions which belong with top government management officials."

Apart from the fusing of public and private roles, the great military expenditures undermine the theory of the government countervail in another and central way. The tens of billions of defense dollars contribute substantially to the centralization of American enterprise, to the dominance of the large corporations. This is because the lion's share of military contracts are placed with a relative handful of great firms. Concentration has marked defense outlays since the second world war. If anything, it is currently increasing rather than declining. During World War II, two-thirds of the military orders were awarded to the 100 largest defense contractors. During Korea, the share of the 100 largest dropped slightly to 64 percent. But in the accounting years from 1958 through 1962, it had risen to nearly three-quarters. The biggest 25 firms alone received more than half of the business during this latest period.

From the standpoint of economic dominance, the most important government dollars are those spent for research and development. These funds finance the search for new knowledge, and new applications of existing knowledge. Firms with the inside track to new technology have the best chance to command the markets of the future. The boxscore of research and development outlays in the United States shows three things. The government provides most of the money for scientific and technological advance. Within the government, the biggest source by far is the military-space-atomic-energy complex, the Cold War agencies. And like defense spending generally, government research and development expenditures are heavily concentrated among a few corporations.*

* In the year 1960–61, for example, the federal government supplied $9.2 billion of the $14 billion spent on research and development. Two years

The flow of federal military and research funds to the large corporations erodes the government's countervailing power in direct as well as indirect ways. The most obvious form of countervail is antitrust action, aimed at reducing the strength of large corporations. But under the stress of the Cold War, the Department of Justice will temper antitrust prosecutions at the request of the Defense Department.

The Justice Department, for example, brought an antitrust action against the American Telephone and Telegraph Co. in 1949. Among other things, the suit asked for the divorce of A T & T from Western Electric, its highly profitable equipment-producing subsidiary. But partly at the request of the Defense Department, Justice officials abandoned this decisive step and permitted A T & T and Western Electric to continue in wedded bliss.

This chapter's description of some of the relations between government and business does not imply acceptance of a crude Marxist formulation that the state is merely an agent of a ruling, capital-owning class. But it does raise serious questions about the equally crude notion that government is and can be an impartial umpire, above the battle, protecting the public interest against contending forces. Professor Earl Lathem wisely suggests that: " 'Government' is merely the device through which advantaged groups perpetuate their advantages, which disadvantaged groups would like to control, but cannot win."

Moreover, federal executive departments and regulatory agencies are not invariably creatures of business. Those govern-

---

earlier, the federal share was $7.2 billion out of $11.1 billion. In a recent period for which figures were compiled, 1959, the government provided private industry with $5.6 billion for research and development or 59 percent of all industrial outlays. Of this sum, $4.2 billion went to the three defense-dominated sectors, aircraft and parts, electrical equipment and communications. Large firms, those with 5000 or more employees, received $5.1 billion or nine dollars out of every ten that the government gave industry for research and development.

mental units with the broadest mandate, those least tied to a particular industry, have frequently and successfully defined and executed a larger interest over business opposition. The Federal Trade Commission, with a roving warrant across all business and no particular client, may be criticized for expending too much energy on trivial cases. But its enforcement of prohibitions against misleading advertising or labeling is a genuine frustration of some businessman's will. The Securities and Exchange Commission could be thought of as an agency with clients, the unconcentrated stock brokers and the concentrated stock underwriters. But it is also an agency that supervises the stock issues of *all* corporations. Again, this breadth of charter may have contributed to the SEC's immunity from the corruption and subservience that have marked other regulatory bodies. Like the FTC, SEC's failings are largely sins of omission rather than commission.

Consider the Antitrust Division of the Justice Department. It may not be able to materially alter the concentrated structure of American business. But it does on occasion interfere with the merger plans of powerful corporations and it does prosecute some of the more glaring instances of price agreement.

There is plenty of play in the American political-economic framework. To contend that a handful of powerful corporations rule unchecked distorts reality. Organized labor may be losing strength and unions may combine with employers in a variety of ways. But this is not to say that unions never oppose corporate managers, never successfully impose their will at both the bargaining table and in the political arena. In the very period that the United Steelworkers and the industry, led by U.S. Steel, were engaged in their wage-price square dance, the industry would have liked to call another tune. It would have preferred smaller or no wage increases to those it granted. The producers took the larger package as a second best. They followed the line of least resistance.

The term "Big Business" itself is a convenient but somewhat misleading shorthand. Industry is not monolithic. Aluminum and steel, commercial banks and savings and loan associations, domestic and international oil producers frequently clash. Within a particular industry, firms have rival and conflicting interests that can't always be resolved by price leadership and tacit market sharing. Finally, corporate officers with the murkiest sense of public responsibility are not indifferent to the potential power of an aroused public opinion. All these stresses and strains modify corporate power.

But the thesis of this and the two preceding chapters is simply this: that for all the strains and offsets that can be seen within and outside the corporate world, the large corporations in the seventh decade of the twentieth century are the strongest repositories of economic power. To depend on their officers' imperfectly formed notions of public interest is no answer; reliance on countervailing power is equally unrealistic. The checks and balances, so dear to the literature and mythology that celebrates what is, should not be exaggerated. Reduced to the simplest terms, this appears to be the position: the economy's key sectors are dominated by the collaborative competition of relatively few large corporations. These firms are reinforced by the administration in Washington. Like its predecessor, the Kennedy regime pursued programs that for the most part harmonized with those sought by the corporations and their principal owners. No matter how well intentioned, the managers of this comparative handful of corporate giants are not likely to run affairs guided by any well-defined notion of public responsibility. Finally, there exists no equally powerful institutions to suggest or impose such a definition on the corporate leaders.

6. The Split-Level Society

Does it really matter? Aren't Americans the richest people in the world? Don't most of us live in affluence or something approaching it? After all, the nation has not suffered a deep depression for a quarter of a century and there is little likelihood that the convulsive slumps of the 1930's or the 1870's will ever be repeated. Since World War II began, employment generally has been high and incomes have been rising. It may be true that the economy is more concentrated than competitive, that politics are business-oriented and that the managers of economic power are nonresponsible and subject only to partial restraint. Perhaps this structure does fall short of the model in an economic text and does trouble theoreticians concerned with linking power to responsibility.

But from a simple material standpoint, does it make much difference? Domestic economic problems no longer absorb public attention and energy. There is an awareness of some anomalies but no sense of urgency. Why would there be? For many Americans, particularly the dominant and articulate majority, material misery is found in India, Haiti or other exotic places. The notion of poverty as an alien strain is reinforced by those who have read the label but not the contents of Galbraith's *The Affluent Society*. Indeed, some of our most thoughtful and sensitive observers are talking of an entirely new set of problems arising from an economy of abundance.

Gerard Piel, publisher of *Scientific American*, asks: "If a fraction of the labor force is capable of supplying an abundance of everything the population needs and wants, then why should the rest of the population have to work for a living?"

Professor Robert Heilbroner declares: "It is no longer sheer fantasy to look ahead to the day when technology will present society with the gift of an immense wealth together with an equally immense vacuum of toil . . . The problem of social existence in a world crammed with goods and emptied of work is still in the future. But already we stand on its outermost threshold."

These are plausible visions, created by imaginative men. But exciting prospects, posing new dilemmas, need not divert us from difficult tasks nearer at hand. The fact is that our present economy is one of paradox, not abundance. Side by side with widespread affluence is deap-seated and pervasive misery.

It is not massive misery, present everywhere and of an equal degree of intensity. But it is much more common than the conventional image of America suggests. Moreover, economic failings in America have consequences outside our borders. The performance of the American economy is important both as a political model and as a market for the poor new nations of the world. These countries are deliberately engaged in a task that is now technically possible for the first time in man's history, wiping out their own poverty. When they succeed, the world will have taken the last great stride towards eliminating physical want. The political structures they develop, the degree to which they value the human personality, will be conditioned in part by the successes and failures of American society.

In sum, the argument here is that our economy is hobbled by its economic structure and that this does matter. The lack of a burning national concern with the present course is explicable. It is also shortsighted and unknowingly cruel.

There is in the United States "an enormous, an unconscionable amount of human suffering." This is the blunt but accurate summary of Michael Harrington, writing of *The Other America*. About one American in five—perhaps 35 million men, women and children—go to bed each night without enough food, clothing and shelter for more than a marginal existence. Hungry, often cold and subject to frequent, uncared for illness, they are caught in a vicious circle with little chance for escape. They lack the schooling, the skills, the stamina and the opportunity to break out. In a society that still cherishes some of the social Darwinists' creed, that regards failure as personal, many of the impoverished fifth see themselves as "rejects, outcasts." For them, Harrington writes, the affluent society "ceases to be a reality or even a hope; it becomes a taunt." Perhaps one-third, more than 10 million, are children under eighteen. Unless the economy's course is changed, these children are likely to repeat their parent's cycle of misery. At a point in economic time when we can produce more than enough for every citizen's needs, poverty in the United States is, as Galbraith said, "a disgrace."

The precise extent of material misery is hard to measure. Moreover, misery is a changing, not a static concept. Our definitions of minimum subsistence rise as standards generally rise. However, recent and expert studies have tended to agree that about 20 percent of the population is living below the poverty line. One careful estimate was made by Professor Lampman of Wisconsin. He defined the poverty line for a family of four as an income of 2500 dollars of 1957 purchasing power. For a single person, it was 1157 of these 1957 dollars. Because of the subsequent rise in prices, the poverty line in 1962 would be about $2700 for a family and nearly $1250 for a single person. Lampman estimated that in 1957 there were 32.2 million persons or 19 percent living below this line.

Leon Keyserling, former chairman of President Truman's Council of Economic Advisers, placed the line in 1960 at an income of $4000 for families and $2000 for single persons. That meant 38 million living in poverty or about 21 percent.

Perhaps the most intensive study was made by the University of Michigan's Institute of Social Research. Their report defined the poverty level as an income equal to nine-tenths of a budget designed for social agencies in New York City. The social agency budget is used as a benchmark of need by private welfare groups. In 1959, this benchmark for a family of four was an income of $4300. How generous was this standard? It permitted the family head $21 a week for all his food, clothing and other personal costs. If his two children were under 12 years old, they could receive no more than $8 a week for all their needs. The family was allowed $125 a month for rent, utilities and other household costs. And this budget, remember, is 11 percent *above* the level that the Michigan team chose as the poverty line. The Michigan group estimated that about 20 percent of the nation's families fell below this line and another 10 percent were right on it.

The Lampman, Keyserling and Michigan estimates differ in detail. But there is a central point of agreement among all three: poverty today afflicts about one in five persons in the United States. As startling as this figure is, it still exaggerates the extent of affluence in America. At or above the poverty line are millions of Americans who are living in what Keyserling aptly calls "deprivation." They are not hungry and they are not necessarily ill-clothed or inhumanly housed. But they are wedged in the margin between poverty and a decent standard of living as the majority of their fellow citizens might define it. These are the persons whose incomes fall below what the Department of Labor describes as a "modest but adequate" standard. The government periodically measures this "level of adequate living" in major cities, the last time in the fall of 1959. The Government experts then defined a modest budget for a typical family of four—a working husband of 38, his wife, their son, 13 and a daughter, 8. To afford the modest standard, the Department concluded they would need an income before taxes ranging from $5370 in Houston to $6567 in Chicago.

This budget does not allow for affluent, let alone riotous living. In Washington, a medium-priced city, it would put the family in a five room apartment renting for about $100 a month. The budget allows $4 a week for reading and recreation and $304 a year for medical care. It provides each of the four persons with about three glasses of milk, one egg and less than half a pound of meat, fish or poultry each day. The mother can buy a vacuum cleaner every 14 years and a toaster every 12 years, a wool blanket every three and a half years and an upholstered chair every 14 years. She can afford each year one cotton dress, one rayon dress and one house dress, and a wool dress every four years. Her husband can buy a top coat every five years and about two shirts a year. The family has a telephone and buys a low-priced used car every three years. They all see a movie every two weeks. The parents can each celebrate their modest life with a one-ounce drink of whiskey every other week.

Keyserling estimated that 39 million Americans who were above the poverty line could not afford even this modest standard in 1960. In all, he concluded about 42 percent of the population—two of five—were below the adequate income line. Similarly, Lampman calculated that 36 percent were beneath this level in 1957. In brief, about 70 million Americans are outside the affluent society and half of them are impoverished.

Numbers are abstractions, symbols to organize experience. The meaning of poverty in America, its taste, smell and feel can better be grasped by a first-hand exploration of a city slum, an Appalachian mining town or a southern sharecroppers' community. But with the growth of suburbs, exurbs and expressways, the impoverished live, as Harrington noted, in an "invisible land," largely out of sight and out of mind of the comfortable majority.

Social workers, newspaper reporters and policemen—those who are professionally compelled to take account of the miserable—have some notion of what life is like for, say, the Puerto Rican family of eight, jammed into two tiny rooms on the upper West Side of New York. The plaster is peeling from the walls, cracked windows leak cold air, an occasional rat threatens the babies and everything is permeated by the nauseating stench of urine and cheap food, that special odor in the dwellings of the urban poor. Sometimes a footnote reference is made to the middle-aged woman in Evansville, Indiana who, with her two children, daily scavenges the fruit throwaway on 10th and Division Streets. Or attention is briefly directed at the jobless anthracite miners in Scranton who now do the housework chores while their wives work in a nearby needlecraft plant.

In 1959, a Special Senate Committee under Senator Eugene McCarthy of Minnesota made an unusual effort to record the atmosphere of poverty in some depressed areas. One witness with a reporter's eye for the concrete was Howard Chambers, the Sheriff of Mingo County in West Virginia. He testified:

> People have nothing to go on. I have had so many men, honest men I have known all my life, come in to me in my office and make the statement that they wouldn't let their children starve if they had to steal. Some actually are stealing food; some are making moonshine. And some men are even going into the mines and cutting wire down, hot wire with juice on it and stealing copper and going out and selling it to provide for their families.

There are people in Mingo County whom I have passed along the garbage dumps where stores throw their garbage out and I have seen little kids eating discarded apples and stuff from the garbage dumps. And it is heartbreaking to see these things.

In Mercer County, West Virginia, the superintendent of schools reported that the only meal "many, many" children have each day is the free school lunch. "And without that, these children would go hungry," he said. In Fayette County by the time many children are fourteen, they have no teeth at all or only decayed stubs. They don't get enough to eat. One Fayette school started a free lunch program in November and by Christmas recess, the children had gained three to five pounds each. After their holiday at home, they lost it all.

A skilled worker in Evansville, Indiana who had been jobless for thirteen months described some of the subtler, corrosive effects of the slide into poverty. His friends began dropping him and his wife. Perhaps it was tact because his friends "knew I could not afford to entertain . . . and they wanted to save us the embarrassment . . . It made us wonder if we were actually forsaken by our friends or if this was true friendship to ignore us." They had a two-year-old daughter. "She began to have nightmares. She tended to be disobedient and just completely frustrated and to just be honest, she just didn't know who was mama around the house."

The editor of the *Mountain Eagle* in Whitesburg, Kentucky told the Senators another story. His friend, a fifty-five-year-old miner from Letcher County, had been out of work for three years although he had hunted for a job as far away as Ohio and Michigan. The miner's unemployment pay was exhausted; his wife cooked in a restaurant and brought home 25 cents a day.

"For some two years, he was forced to sit in idleness at

home, watching the health of his children deteriorate from lack of enough food—watching their clothes wear out—with no money to replace them," the editor said.

Then the ex-miner calculated that if he died his family would receive social security payments.

"And so as a Christmas present to his wife and his eight children, the man took out his shotgun and calmly killed himself. It was the best Christmas present he knew how to give. Living he was of no help to his family. By dying he could feed them."

These glimpses of the plight of a handful suggest that the poor generally suffer from some special characteristics. Every student of contemporary poverty has stressed that this is indeed the case. The impoverished are concentrated among the aged, the disabled, the non-white, the unschooled, the jobless and the single women—divorced, widowed or deserted—with children. These special marks have led to a belief that a general rise in the economy, an advance in over-all living standards will do little to shrink the ranks of the poverty-stricken. Gains in national income, it is argued, would still leave untouched the unskilled Negro slum dweller or the unemployed fifty-year-old miner.

Galbraith, for example, contended that poverty in the United States can be divided into two classes. One is case poverty, stemming from "some quality peculiar to the individual or family involved" like poor health, a mental defect or insufficient schooling. The other is island poverty, those trapped in distressed communities around the worn-out coal seams in West Virginia or the dying textile towns of New England. If Galbraith is right, increases in national production and incomes by themselves won't help much. Only special programs, tailored to the particular disabilities of the two classes, would cut deeply into poverty.

Lampman, however, closely examined Galbraith's thesis

and concluded that he was wrong. Between 1947 and 1957, when incomes and output generally were rising at a fairly rapid pace, the ranks of the impoverished were reduced sharply. Over this decade, the percentage of those in the poverty class fell more than a quarter, from 26 percent of the population to 19 percent.

Rising incomes, better schooling and increased job opportunities, Lampman deduced, drew people out of the impoverished islands and helped cure the defects that had marked some "cases." In other words, a growing economy will of itself cut into poverty. At most, Lampman conceded that economic growth alone will in the future tend to reduce poverty at a "slightly slower" pace than in the first postwar decade.

Lampman's empirical findings have a logical ring. A faster growing economy won't change the color of a Negro's skin. But as job openings increase, he is less likely to run into discriminatory hiring practices that bar him from employment. Similarly, the sons of the impoverished Alabama farmer are much more likely to leave their island if they have a genuine prospect of a job in the city.

Growing production and incomes won't by themselves do much for the aged and the disabled. But society will be much more willing to pay for special benefits to lift the disadvantaged from poverty if these payments are subtracted from rising rather than static incomes. Similarly, programs to retrain the unskilled, expand schooling and provide day nurseries for the children of single women all cost money. Self-interested opposition to these plans is likely to diminish if they can be financed from increased incomes. If in the future, the affluent society expresses more than a verbal or token concern for the large number of impoverished, an expanding economy offers the best setting in which to take the needed steps. A rapid rate of growth is the swiftest route to reduce material misery in the United States.

Perhaps the most obvious way to slice into poverty is to

provide jobs for all those willing and able to work. It is the peculiar distinction of the postwar economy that it has been plagued by a slowly rising tide of unemployment. Like poverty, this joblessness has not been a massive affliction. It in no way resembles the desperate 'thirties when as many as 13 million workers, a quarter of the labor force, were out of work. But unlike poverty which was shrinking during the first years of postwar growth, the percentage of unemployed has been steadily creeping upward. In each business cycle since the war, from one peak of business activity to the next, the percentage of those at work has been declining. During the first cycle, from 1948 to 1953, the jobless rate averaged 4.2 percent; in the next, to 1957, the rate inched up to 4.4 percent; in the next, to 1960, it climbed to 5.9 percent. At this writing, the latest cycle has not yet run its course. But in the period from the 1960 peak through the second quarter of 1963, the rate had risen a little again. Over this last three year stretch unemployment averaged 6.0 percent.

Another way of looking at this strange phenomenon is to mark the level of unemployment in the months of keenest business activity, just before the economy turned down into recession. Here again, the trend line reveals a climbing rate of joblessness. The first postwar boom reached a high point in November 1948. In that month, unemployment was 3.7 percent.* The next boom reached a crest in July 1953 and unemployment fell to 2.6 percent. The third crested in July, 1957 and unemployment rose to 4.2 percent; the fourth advance halted in May, 1960 and unemployment stood at 5.2 percent. When the 1960 peak was reached, a milestone of sorts was established. It marked the first time since 1937 that a wave of economic advance had failed to pull the jobless rate below or close to 4 percent.

The recent history has been the most depressing. From the

---

* Because the government changed its technique of measurement, this figure is not exactly comparable with those that follow.

beginning of 1958 through the first half of 1963, the jobless rate stuck at 5 percent or more in every month but one. This meant that all during these five and a half years, at least one person in twenty who was actively looking for work could not find it. This has been the longest period of prolonged unemployment since the 1930's. Over this dismal stretch, the number of persons counted as unemployed at any time has averaged more than 4 million.*

The slowly rising tide of jobless has raised some disturbing questions about the nature of work in a technologically advanced society. These questions challenge the belief that unemployment can or should be solved by an expanding economy. One such theory assumes a society of abundance already exists, a society in which there are enough goods for all. This implies that the real problem is not supplying jobs but incomes or claims on these abundant goods.

Piel, for example, speaks of a coming "workless" world which must confront "the specter of universal leisure." Galbraith argues that increased output won't mean "more food for the hungry, more clothing for the cold and more houses for the homeless" but merely "satisfies the craving for more elegant automobiles, more exotic food, more erotic clothing, more elaborate entertainment."

Thus, he contends, "When men are unemployed, society

* The reported levels of unemployment actually understate the economy's failure to provide jobs. When unemployment is high and prolonged, many persons are discouraged from looking for work. These people are not counted as either employed or unemployed. They are statistically invisible. Thus, the Council of Economic Advisers estimated that in 1962 there were 800,000 persons omitted from the reckoning who would normally be at work or looking for work. They were simply not counted because they stayed at home. This group is one-fifth as large as the 4 million who were officially recorded as jobless that year. In addition, the rate of unemployment does not take account of those who are forced to work part-time because the economy isn't strong enough to provide them with the full-time work they seek. In the official statistics, a man is counted as employed if he works as little as one paid hour in a week. The number of involuntary part-time workers in 1962 was 1.3 million.

does not miss the goods they do not produce. The loss here is marginal. But the men who are without work *do* miss the income they no longer earn."

So, Galbraith would weaken the tie between output and incomes by adopting a sliding scale of unemployment payments. As the rate of unemployment and the difficulty of finding a job rises, he would increase the amount of the cash payments to the jobless; as unemployment fell, the payments would decline.

Here are two perceptive observers who suggest that the concern with jobs is already or will soon become obsolete. The trouble with this idea—apart from the fact that the society of abundance is not yet at hand—is, as Galbraith himself recognizes, "the normal, if surprising preference of people for work" over idleness.

Even if there is a change in the deeply imbedded attitude that income should be a reward for work, it is not likely that most people would choose to do nothing. As Thorstein Veblen sensed, there is in men an "instinct of workmanship," a creative impulse, a hunger for purposeful achievement. This in itself is a powerful reason for insisting that no economy fully satisfies human needs unless it provides jobs for all who seek them. This is not to argue that all jobs satisfy the instinct of workmanship or the craving for creation. Indeed, the meaningless content of much modern work accounts for some of the alienation that social psychologists have observed. Perhaps the greatest benefit that a society of abundance will bring is the elimination of unsatisfying labor and an increase in jobs that fulfill the creative urge. But to contend that the problem of unemployment can be reduced merely by supplying claims on goods for those without work conflicts with a driving force in man's nature. Somewhere Freud says that work is the best cure for neurosis. His insight is one that economists, still largely captives of a primitive Benthamite psychology, would do well to respect. Sheriff Chambers of Mingo County understands this. Talking of his jobless constituents, he said: "They are honest people and good people, and they don't want a handout from the government. They don't want a handout from anyone. They want an honest living; they want something to do to work and make an honest living."

During the 1960's, the problem of unemployment threatens to become worse. Because of the shape of the population curve, the economy must increase its job-creating ability merely to hold unemployment where it is now. This is the decade in which the great war and postwar boom in babies will be swelling the army of job seekers. The Labor Department estimates that 26 million youths will be looking for their first job in the 1960's, by far the greatest number in the nation's history.

To be sure, older persons retire from the work force each year, too. But on balance, the government estimates that there will be an additional 1,300,000 job seekers every year of the decade. Moreover, in the period directly ahead, this total is likely to be even higher. Those who stayed on the sidelines in recent years because jobs were scarce may now seek their normal place in the labor market.

At the same time, technological change, increased productivity, automation, the replacement of men by machines—call it what you will—inexorably reduces the number of workers needed to produce existing levels of output. Although there is good reason to believe that technological unemployment or automation unemployment has not added a new dimension to the problem, the fact is that innovation does go on. Jobs that men once performed are now done by machines. If the pace of this change keeps step with that of the postwar period, another two million jobs will disappear every year in the 1960's.

Putting these two forces together—the rise in the labor

force and the steady march of technology—the economy will have to provide about 3.3 million added jobs each year simply to contain unemployment at its present, unsatisfactory level. As President Kennedy said in his 1963 Economic Report, "We need to run just to keep pace and run swiftly to gain ground . . ."

Just as some students of poverty mistakenly concluded that expanding production and rising incomes will do little to help the impoverished, a related school contends that a growing economy will not make substantial inroads on the rising army of unemployed. These theorists believe that there is a "hard core" of jobless whose number is slowly growing as the economy is transformed.

In this view, the new technology has reshaped the economy's structure. It has placed a premium on skills, on education, on white collar jobs. As the new machines and new industries rise, they leave behind the unskilled, the inadequately schooled and the blue collar worker. Along with the new technology go changing tastes and changing demands. These changes swell the battalions of unwanted coal miners, textile workers and the like. The inability of such workers to fill the new jobs opening in electronics, government work and services like finance, real estate or recreation condemns them to the ranks of the continuing unemployed. As the economy grows, it will grow in these sectors—services, government and technologically advanced industries. It will not automatically open up jobs for the hard core of unemployed. Of itself, economic expansion won't be much help.

This thesis not only attempts to indicate the best lines for future policy; it is an effort to explain what has been happening. It says in effect that the rising tide of unemployment is essentially due to the new technical shape of the economy, to a growing wave of unemployables. It implies that there has not been a universal shortage of jobs but a shortage of properly trained workers for the economy's new kind of work. In sum, the theory holds that the slow climb in unemployment is caused by too many square worker pegs for round job holes.

There is something in this notion of a hard core of unemployables, but much less than its proponents claim. So far, there have been two serious attempts to measure its validity. Both reached the same conclusion: hard core or structural unemployment is not rising. It cannot account for the *increasing* levels of unemployment. Put another way, the two studies agree that there is a group among the jobless who won't find work without special help. But this group is not growing and the cause of higher unemployment must be found elsewhere.

One study was made by James W. Knowles, staff director of the Congressional Joint Economic Committee, with the help of Edward P. Kalachek. They examined the rise of unemployment between 1957 and 1960. Among other things, they found that the rate of unemployment had climbed in all occupational groups, not just those affected by automation. This is one major indication that the hard core explanation doesn't fit.

Just as important, they discovered that during this period the number of vacant jobs shrank in every major occupational category. If the hard core theorists were right, the number of job openings should have been climbing, or at least not falling as rapidly in the skilled, white collar areas as in the unskilled, blue collar sectors. But this didn't happen. Jobs were drying up across the board. In other words, rising unemployment could not be blamed on the fact that the wrong workers were looking for jobs. There just weren't enough jobs. In the words of the two economists, "if an adequate number of jobs had been available, workers would have sought them out, regardless of their geographic or industrial concentration."

During the early months of President Kennedy's administration, his Council of Economic Advisers also tested the hard core argument by comparing 1957 and 1960. Again, if the structural theorists were right, unemployment should have been rising fastest among women, older workers, in depressed areas, among the unskilled and the non-white. In fact, unemployment was rising in all groups at about the same pace. For example, between 1957 and 1960, the rate of unemployment for professional and sales workers rose 42 percent; for operatives or semiskilled workers, only 27 percent and for laborers, 33 percent. Similarly, the jobless rate in finance, insurance and real estate rose 33 percent but in manufacturing only 24 percent.

"There is little evidence," the Council said, "that current unemployment is unusually concentrated in particular compartments of the labor force, whether age, sex, color, marital status or education. Nor can the current level of unemployment be attributed to certain industry or occupation groups. There is little evidence that current unemployment is primarily a result of unfavorable changes in the labor force. The evidence is that our high over-all rate of unemployment comes from higher unemployment rates group by group, category by category, throughout the labor force."

The two reports should have fatally wounded the belief that hard core unemployment is rising. That they did not demonstrates the persistence of economic myth, particularly the myth that suggests the economy as a whole is sound and requires only patchwork programs. For if there is no increasing core of unemployables, it means that rising unemployment can be reversed only by measures to lift the entire economy. In other words, the army without jobs can be reduced by a growing economy that supplies more work generally. The only careful studies of the problem agree that the mounting tide of joblessness stems from a lack of demand for goods and services. In economists' jargon, demand is not simply a desire for more, but desire backed by cash. If this economic demand were stronger, production would be increased to satisfy it and this extra production would mean the hiring of more workers.

The studies do not dismiss hard core unemployment, the workers who would find it difficult to get jobs even in a stronger economy. There is such a group and its members require special kinds of help. But concern for the unschooled, unskilled, disabled and other disadvantaged workers "ought not to divert our attention from the real cause of weakness in 1961's labor market," the Council wrote, "and that is inadequate demand." In the same vein, Knowles and Kalachek tersely concluded: "Indications of inadequate demand are present in a host of economic time series."

Like the problem of poverty, the glut of rising unemployment can be dissolved in a stronger, faster growing economy. Neither will disappear completely without special treatment, but both will be drastically reduced if output and incomes grow at a more rapid pace. Moreover, the special help needed to relieve the plight of those workers who can be assigned legitimately to the hard core category will be undertaken more readily in an expanding economy. Unemployables can be employed if they are healthy, literate and trained. This means programs of health care, elementary schooling and vocational training. These programs are much more likely to be started on the needed scale, on something more than a token level, if they impose no added burden on the rest of the population. Like the special programs required to wipe out the last vestiges of poverty, they will meet far less resistance if they can be paid from taxes on increased incomes rather than by redistributing the existing pie.

If the hard core theory can't be sustained, there is still a popular conviction that something new has been added to the problem of unemployment. This is automation. Certainly the new machines and processes are dramatic—magical computers, virtually workerless oil refineries, plants that automatically perform 500 operations on auto engines. Have the studies by Knowles and the Council passed over the new technology too lightly? President Kennedy himself suggested as much. "The major domestic challenge of the Sixties," he told a news conference in February 1962, is "to maintain full employment at a time when automation of course is replacing men."

Whether or not the President probed the problem's deepest roots, at least automation is clearly a new dimension in technology. In 1955, some astute members of the Congressional Joint Economic Committee said:

"We don't know what all this will add up to, but we might very well be wrong to think of it as simply 'more of the same' technology which has always characterized American industry."

Piel has identified the essential change. The older technology of the Industrial Revolution, from steam engine to electric power, replaced the "biologically generated energy of human muscle." The new technology of automation performs the work of the human nervous system. The new tools—computers, transfer devices and automatic controls—are self-regulating and self-correcting. They behave much like a sensing, thinking man.

This technological breakthrough has been so dramatic in industries like coal mining that it has created a popular image of robot-like machines displacing men. As long as attention is confined to special cases, automation unemployment has a flavor of reality. But the notion that automation is the source of *rising* joblessness begins to disappear when the economy as a whole is examined.

To measure technological displacement throughout a society, economists turn to the concept of the "productivity of labor." The productivity of labor measures how much imput of labor is required for a given output of product. Since the skills, the machines and the organization of work are constantly changing in a modern economy, the crucial question is how rapidly is productivity increasing. For example, assume that five workers could produce 50 widgets an hour in 1960. During the year, the widget industry began using some new machines, its workers were better trained and its management found more efficient ways of running their plants. As a result, the five workers in 1961 could turn out 55 widgets an hour. The productivity of widget labor had increased 10 percent in a year.

By comparing changes in the productivity of labor over different periods of time, economists can test whether automation has created a new unemployment problem. If it has, we would expect that the yearly gains in labor productivity would have risen sharply in the recent past.

The evidence, however, points the other way. The recent gains in productivity have been in line with historic trends. One set of studies indicating as much was made by the government's Bureau of Labor Statistics. Leaving out farm workers whose productivity has shot forward at astronomical rates and government workers who are less directly involved in the automation question, this is what the BLS found: Over the half century between 1909 and 1961, workers increased their hourly production of goods an average of 2.1 percent each year. In other words, if 10 workers could produce 1000 units of all commodities in one day of one year, they would turn out on the average 1021 units the next year. This rate of labor productivity was greater in some periods than in others. In the depression years it was the same 2.1 per cent. But since the end of World War II, the average pace rose to 2.7 percent. Was this because of automation?

Probably not. After the first World War, the yearly gain in labor productivity was just as rapid, 2.7 percent, and there was no automation then. Moreover, even bigger gains were made immediately after World War II. But between 1950 and 1961, the yearly pace fell back to 2.4 percent although automation was then spreading more widely throughout industry.

Proponents of automation unemployment could retort that this is not conclusive. The real question is what happened in manufacturing and particularly to production workers. Since World War II, manufacturing industries have been hiring relatively more sales, clerical, professional and technical workers. They don't directly increase the output of widgets, automobiles or steel. As a result, these nonproduction workers drag down the reported increases in labor productivity.

But Knowles of the Joint Economic Committee has explored this question and his results also provide little comfort to those who want to blame mounting unemployment on automation. Knowles specifically examined the productivity increases of production workers in manufacturing. Between 1909 and 1960, the yearly gain averaged 3.1 percent. The rate did rise sharply to 4.3 percent between 1948 and 1960. But this advance was not as spectacular as that of the pre-automation era between 1920 and 1929 when productivity jumped 5.6 percent a year.*

The fact that worker productivity rose rapidly after both World War I, when there was no automation, and after World War II, when there was, does lead to another conclusion. The great advances tend to come when industry is running its plants reasonably near to capacity. Productivity slows down in slumps when a greater portion of the plants are idle.

But at this point, it cannot be said that automation has noticeably accelerated gains in productivity. It is certainly

* Nothing in economics is clear-cut and diehard believers in automation unemployment can find some help in Knowles' data. The productivity of manufacturing production workers was rising steadily if slowly all during the postwar period. However, these advances were still well below the remarkable gains of the 1920's.

changing the work process. And, like technological change in the past, it is reducing the man-hours required to turn out a given amount of work in some industries and some occupations. As in the past, too, this will add to the ranks of the unemployed unless the economy grows to absorb the displaced workers. But the pace of this displacement does not appear to have broken into fresh ground. If automation can't be blamed for rising unemployment, the cause again must be a lack of total demand.

This is not to say that automation is not creating some new employment problems. The Joint Economic Committee members who perceived a qualitative change were correct. In several industries and occupations that once provided outlets for semiskilled youths, jobs are shrinking. The computer that can do the work of a score of file clerks in an insurance office may not cost any regular employee her job; but young girls fresh from high school are likely to find fewer openings. Similarly, an auto plant may reassign its work so that a new transfer device won't lead to a single firing; but young men coming from vocational school will have less chance to work on the assembly line. "The problem becomes not the worker who is fired but the worker who is not hired," says Professor Walter Buckingham. "The unions call this 'silent firing.' "

Moreover, as the new technology widens its reach, it tends to squeeze workers into white collar jobs and service industries. In many of these occupations, the pay is less than in semiskilled factory jobs. Finally, automation is changing the content of work itself. In factories, the new jobs are generally cleaner and more like office work. But this is a mixed blessing. Workers are more widely separated than on the assembly line and lose the satisfaction of human contact. Automation in the office brings similar problems. The operator of a large computer has less control over the pace of her work and is more subject to the impersonal supervision of a self-regulating machine than the conventional file clerk or typist. In both blue and white collar jobs, automation may well be increasing the tensions of work.

Just as expanding demand, production, jobs and income bite into poverty and reduce unemployment, so too many of the special problems of automation will be relieved by faster growth. Put another way, a malfunctioning economy that advances slowly or not at all, where output and employment are inhibited by the price policies of large giants, will heighten the strains of the new technology. A company faced with rising demand will be much more likely to adjust to the needs of its workers the rate at which new technology is put in place. Such a firm will also be better equipped to retrain displaced workers for other tasks, to protect the incomes of those seeking new jobs or to provide those nearing retirement with a continued claim on goods. Layoff pay, supplements to unemployment compensation, inducements to early retirement can all be financed more easily from a rising than a static level of income.

In the same way, an expanding economy as a whole can afford much more generous treatment for workers displaced from firms too small to carry on such ambitious programs. Indeed, it is clear that the problems and solutions of poverty, unemployment and automation overlap to a large extent. All can be dealt with much more easily in the environment of a growing economy.

"Automation will accelerate the development of a new leisure class . . . democratic in composition and temper . . . With increasing time to himself, man is more than ever in need of improved taste, more diversified interests, more constructive social values, a more active sense of citizenship, and higher individual ideals."

This lofty quotation from Henry M. Wriston is empty rhetoric to the elderly pensioner living alone on the average social security benefit of $82 a month, the high school graduate who has been looking for work unsuccessfully for months

and the fifty-year-old steel worker who has just been laid off.
But in an economy of increasing output and incomes, it could
have some content.

A faster rate of economic growth, a quickening in the yearly
gains in the production of goods and services, is often discussed in the context of the Cold War. The Soviet and American economies are likened to a pair of marathon runners whose
ultimate position depends on growth rates. Apart from this
dubious kind of gamesmanship, there are important domestic
reasons for seeking a faster pace. It is the most direct way to
wipe out the misery of poverty and the indignity of unemployment.

On almost any standard, the economy's growth has been
stunted since the end of the Korean War. The nation has
been limping along at a sluggish rate that isn't fast enough to
provide jobs for all who want them or to continue the inroads
into poverty made right after World War II. The Russians
aside, the United States suffered the slowest rate of growth
during the 1950's of any advanced nation except Great Britain.

Here is the statistical record. For most of the twentieth
century, through booms and slumps, war and peace, the nation's average yearly growth was 2.9 percent. That is, the
annual gain in gross national product, the dollar value of all
goods and services, rose an average of 2.9 percent between
1909 and 1960.

Immediately after the war, when consumers were flush with
wartime savings and starved for civilian goods, the economy
spurted. Between 1947 and 1953, the yearly gains averaged
4.6 percent. This was nearly 60 percent faster than the historic pace. To be sure this high rate was boosted by the heavy
demand of the Korean War, but it showed what the economy
was capable of doing.*

---

* A sceptical reader, recalling the rapid rise in prices after World War II,
might question whether the postwar growth rate was an illusion. Was the
faster pace simply the result of higher price tags on the same physical volume

However, between 1953 and 1962, the growth pace slowed down and even fell below the long-term trend. The advance averaged only 2.7 percent a year. During that time the economy moved forward in fits and starts; mild slumps were succeeded by unimpressive recoveries. If a rate of 4.5 percent had been maintained in these years, output in 1962 would have been a healthy $650 billion instead of the $554 billion that was produced. And during those nine years, the nation would have been able to dispose altogether of an extra $392 billion in dollars of 1962 purchasing power.

If the economy continues to advance in this halting fashion, even if the historic 2.9 percent pace is maintained, the tide of unemployment will rise higher. Recall that in this decade about 3.3 million new jobs must be created each year merely to hold the jobless at their present level. Growth at only the traditional rate will swell the army of youths unsuccessfully seeking their first job or the experienced and idle workers displaced by technological advance.

The intimate tie between growth and unemployment is a logical, not merely a statistical connection. The basic sources of economic growth, of gains in output, are increased resources and increased efficiency in the use of these resources.* Or, in simpler terms, the more we work, the more we have to work with and the better we work, the more we produce. Labor itself is a prime resource and labor productivity is another term for efficiency. The growth in population expands

---

of goods and services? The answer is no. The rates of growth discussed here are "real rates," computed in dollars of the same purchasing power. In other words, assume that the total output in one year was valued at $500 billion and output the following year at $520 billion. But prices rose that year an average of 2 percent. The "real" gain in output, then, was not $20 billion but only $9.6 billion. Two percent of the $520 billion or $10.4 billion was not a real gain but merely reflected higher prices. So, the growth over the year is not recorded as 4 percent but only 2 percent.

* Resources here means not only our natural and human resources but also our capital stock of plants and machines. So, increased capital investment is another source of faster growth.

the resource of labor; labor productivity or efficiency increases fastest when the economy is booming, not when plants are idle.

A leading student of growth in the American economy, Edward F. Denison of the Brookings Institution, has concluded that "maintenance of a high rate of employment is the most promising single means open to us to influence the future growth rate favorably." If unemployment remains high, he warns, it will be hard to resist demands for policies that will choke off economic growth. Organized labor has already begun to raise one such demand with its talk of a shorter work week. The more that working time is reduced, the less output there will be and the slower the economy will grow. To be sure, this line of reasoning assumes that there are or will be jobs available for all who seek work. Its logic evaporates if shorter or zero working hours are involuntarily imposed on workers. Then there is no loss of output from shorter hours, but a redistribution of the available working time. However, if hours are cut more than usual now, and this reduction is maintained in a future economy of full employment, total production will be less.

High unemployment, Denison observes, also discourages investment and research into new technology, two important sources of growth. It also discourages workers from leaving farms and depressed areas where they are idle or wastefully employed and seeking more productive jobs in new industries. It stiffens union resistance against abandoning wasteful work practices and builds up opposition to labor-saving machines. Finally, large jobless rolls lead to demands for protection against more efficiently produced foreign goods.

In sum, Denison says that "high employment is almost a necessary precondition to acceptance and adoption of policies to carry us along . . . to accelerated growth."

In a society in which so many are affluent, some thoughtful

critics are asking whether faster growth is a worthwhile goal. We have now or could have a surfeit of goods, they argue. We could eliminate poverty simply by redistributing some of the claims on goods, taking from the affluent and giving to the deprived. The Michigan study of poverty calculated that only $10 billion a year—less than two percent of our output —separates those below the poverty line from a subsistence level.

However attractive such a notion may seem, the resistance to a reshuffling of incomes would be enormous. A higher rate of growth can achieve the same end at much less pain. Moreover, a better division of wealth is not likely to have much effect on unemployment, particularly as the labor force expands.* If we are to provide jobs for all who want them, we must grow more rapidly.

Another line of criticism is aimed at the indiscriminate concept of economic goods. Growth, it is argued, is a measure of increases in the economy's quantitative output, its production of television sets, automobiles, ski lodges, schools, outlays for teaching, books, mink coats, and a whole complex of undifferentiated goods and services. What matters, it is said, is the quality of an economy, not some crude measure of its quantity that makes equal a dollar spent on scholarship and a dollar spent on electric toothbrushes.

This is not a simple argument to answer. The trouble is, whose taste shall govern? Mine, for scotch, sociology and sports or yours for ties, travel and television. If we can't agree on an arbiter of taste or quality, at least all of our desires are likely to be better satisfied in a growing rather than a stagnant economy. Faster growth may lead to the production of much that you and I would regard as crude or wasteful (although

* A more equal distribution of incomes might have some effect, however. It would put more purchasing power in the hands of those who spend the most and less in the hands of those who save the most. Thus, redistribution would increase demand for goods, production and employment.

others will put an equally low value on the things we buy),
but it will also bring about an increase in those things we do
want. In other words, the key to improving quality may lie in
increasing quantity.*

Still another criticism centers around the race-with-Russia
argument. Since the Soviets start from a lower level of production and can impose their will by fiat, aren't we engaging
in a meaningless competition with a society that can better
mobilize its resources for a more impressive showing in a
race for crude economic growth?

Again, this argument can't be dismissed out of hand. But
even if we choose to abandon the competition, others will
keep score. The new nations struggling to wipe out mass poverty are not likely to imitate slavishly either the Soviet or the
American pattern. But the institutions they develop, their
mode of living, will inevitably be affected by the economic
performance of the two giants.

Without laboring the point, the world in general and the
United States in particular will probably be a more comfortable place if these new nations take as their own the central
Western value, respect for the unique personality of each individual man. While this nation's economic performance sometimes seems to affront that value, it remains the core of the
Western tradition. It is likelier to take root in the rest of the
world if it is realized at home in a material as well as a political or even more abstract sense.

At a more concrete level, faster economic growth at home
will better serve the poor nations abroad. These new countries
all export raw materials and some are beginning to produce

* This is not an entirely satisfactory answer. Increased output may also mean
greater traffic jams, more crowding in cities, heavier smogs, more billboarded
highways, greater destruction of pleasant neighborhoods and the like. Unless
some social mechanism is designed that compels economic decision makers to
consider the quality of modern life, more rapid growth will not be an
unmitigated blessing.

goods requiring little capital, like textiles. They need the markets of the developed world for their coffee, rice, jute, cloth, oil, iron ore, rubber, copper and much more. These exports will pay for imports of heavier machinery, skills and capital that will enable them to escape from backwardness. The faster our economy grows, the more it will buy abroad, the lower will be our barriers to foreign goods and the better we will be able to afford special devices like international price propping agreements and direct foreign aid to raise the incomes of the commodity producing nations.

This brief excursion from poverty at home to the poor abroad appears to have wandered a long way from the earlier themes of domestic conservatism, concentration, conscience and countervails. There is, however, a genuine connection.

The argument has been that poverty, employment and growth are intimately entangled. This chapter has suggested that higher employment and faster growth depend in great measure on increased demand, on greater cash outlays by government, business and consumers. Chapter 2 reviewed the Kennedy administration's persuasive analysis that the present mix of federal spending and tax revenues is holding back growth and employment. Thus, the Administration attempted to release the brake and increase demand by reducing taxes and enlarging military outlays.

An important assumption underlies this approach. It is that the federal expenditures and the tax-freed dollars placed in consumer and corporation hands will constitute real purchasing power. If the two techniques increase real demand, there will be more orders for goods, increased investment to expand industries and more employment. A base will be laid for other policies to stimulate growth like maintaining the length of the work week.

But if the extra dollars are eaten up by higher prices, there will be no increased demand, orders, investment and jobs. If the federal stimulus simply inspires businessmen to place bigger price tags on the existing output, nothing will be gained. With so much plant capacity idle and so many workers jobless, the Administration insisted that there would be no pressure on prices. In a competitive economy, this would be a perfectly reasonable conclusion.

But ours is an economy of concentration in which the leaders of key industries are exempt to some extent from the discipline of the market. In the absence of new institutional arrangements to define and promote responsible behavior, corporate managers might decide to raise their target rates of return. Or some unions might take advantage of the initial burst in money demand to seek wage increases greater than the gains in productivity. And this in turn could induce concentrated corporations to lift prices by an offsetting or even greater amount. As prices rise, the extra demand flowing from the government's measures would melt away. They would create paper increases with little effect on jobs or growth.

This is not some bleak fantasy created from a predilection for despair. Something very much like this took place after President Eisenhower cut taxes in 1954. In the years that followed, prices rose, and after a strong but brief spurt in the economy, so did unemployment. The stable prices of more recent years went hand in hand with even higher unemployment and flattened growth.

Given the nonresponsible nature of powerful corporations, it could happen again. Indeed, even before the Kennedy tax cuts were enacted, the steel industry legislated a price increase in the spring of 1963 and other major industries indicated they might follow this lead.

The answer then to the question at the beginning of this chapter is "Yes." It does matter. In summary form, the state of affairs is as follows: Despite the spread of affluence and near-affluence in our society, there is also an impressive amount of poverty and deprivation. It exists at a time when unemployment and its consequent indignities is rising and threatens to rise further. At the same time, growth in the economy, the prime source for eradicating material want and unemployment and a force with crucial implications for the rest of the world, is stunted. All of these unhappy events feed on each other.

There is a stock of well-known remedies for all these ills. But our political-economic structure, built around corporate concentration, both contributes to our present plight and threatens to transform cures into placebos. This structure's potential for damage needs closer examination. One special case of the general proposition lies in the complex of problems linked to a disarming economy. Disarmament, of course, is essentially a concern of international politics and hinges on the relations of the great powers. However, domestic attitudes toward disarmament are conditioned to an unusual extent by the peculiar economy that has evolved in the United States. For this reason, a look at the economics of disarmament is now in order.

7. The Two Half-Truths
of Disarmament

Nor are there any insurmountable economic obstacles to disarmament for the capitalist countries, including the United States.
— Reply of the Union of Soviet Socialist Republics to a United Nations inquiry.

Nevertheless, given the existing situation, a large security budget *is* an antideflationary force.
— Charles J. Hitch, Defense Department Comptroller and Roland N. McKean, Rand Corporation.

SOONER OR LATER, the United States is likely to level off and then reduce its rising tide of arms spending.

This is not a forecast that can be buttressed with an impressive array of fact or even logic. Reference to the past, always an uncertain guide, is perhaps even less reliable in a nuclear age. The logic that should flow from the prospect of thermonuclear holocaust could be overmatched by the dark, irrational drives that are as much man's nature as reason. Perhaps disarmament should more candidly be called a hope, rather than a prediction.

But despite the interminable, tedious and largely unsuccessful series of disarmament negotiations, a drift of sentiment away from pursuit of the arms race was more and more evi-

dent by the early 1960's. After each cycle of hope and dis-
appointment at the conference table had run its course in the
recent past, there was some evidence that a residue of gain
had been deposited, that the modest goal of a step-by-step
reduction in military outlays was a little closer. There was
increasing reason to think that military budgets, currently
absorbing about $120 billion a year of the globe's resources or
nearly as much as the entire annual income of all the underdeveloped nations, will be cut back. At the same time, there
is virtually no prospect that peace will break out overnight.
Indeed, disarming could very well begin with unwritten, limited understandings between the two great powers before any
explicit agreements are reached.

This is not the place to analyze more closely the prospects
or shape of any particular agreement. But an examination of
the economics of arming and disarming is appropriate for two
reasons. It illuminates some of the dilemmas of a concentrated corporate structure and, in its own right, might dispel
some of the illusions about arms and the economy. This last
in turn could affect the prospects of an agreement to disarm.
According to the unanimous opinion of a representative
group of United Nations consultants, such an agreement
would be "an unqualified blessing to all mankind."

As long as the lurking fear remains that American prosperity depends on arms spending, that cutbacks would bring
recession or depression, the domestic political opposition to
disarmament will probably be strong enough by itself—apart
from the balkiness of the Soviet Union—to prevent it. There
is no blinking the fact that important politicians, industrialists, labor leaders and many businessmen and workers generally are nakedly fearful of their economic future in a disarming world. Indeed, Edward Kennedy successfully cam-
paigned for the Senate on the thinly disguised promise to
increase material well-being in Massachusetts by bringing

the state more defense business. On the other hand, a simple assertion that the economy can function smoothly if the arms budget suddenly disappears is wishful thinking. The Machinists' union members on Long Island who raised a storm over the cancellation of Republic Aviation's Thunderchief contract knew better. Moreover, the very real economic and political problems posed by disarmament are intensified by the limping economy itself, the economy of rising unemployment and slow growth described in the last chapter. Conversely, a growing economy with jobs for all can soften and shrink many of the difficulties.*

The American economy today is heavily supported by arms spending. Defense is, by a wide margin, the nation's biggest industry. In the year ending June 30, 1964, the government expects to buy $56 billion of goods and services for the military. This will absorb nearly one-tenth of our total output. By 1965, an estimated 7.4 million persons will be serving the defense establishment directly or indirectly. This total includes 3 million in the armed forces, 1.2 million civilians working for the government in the Defense Department or defense-related agencies and 3.2 million employed in industries turning out military goods or producing goods in other

---

* Throughout this discussion, I am assuming that disarmament means a reduction in military spending. However, in the contemporary Orwellian world there is another school for whom, as Hitch and McKean have observed, "disarmament sometimes means armament." Professor Thomas C. Schelling of Harvard is the leading proponent of the view that arms control not only may not reduce but could increase military spending. In somewhat simplified form, the kind of control that Schelling discusses involves invulnerable forces capable of destroying enemy populations as a 'guarantee' against enemy attack. Hitch and McKean call this "stable and effective deterrence." Schelling prefers the phrase "balance of prudence" to "balance of fear." The notion that stability and rational decision making can exist in a world posed on the brink of universal disaster is one that historians and psychologists, among others, might question. In any case, this form of reciprocal terror is not what I mean by disarmament. Unlike Humpty Dumpty, I am using the word in its common sense to mean a reduction in weapons and weapons spending.

industries that flow into the military stream. Thus, nearly one worker in ten owes his livelihood to arms outlays.

It is this enormous outlay that accounts for the economic fears over a reduction in arms spending. As the unsentimental team of Hitch and McKean have observed: "When government spends such an amount for national security (or for anything else), it tends to buoy up total spending. The existence of this demand makes a deficiency of total demand less probable." Or, in plain English, a prop so big is a sturdy bulwark against a deep slump. The equally unsentimental purchasers of corporate shares have a profound appreciation of the importance of military outlays. In recent years, the stock market has often slumped on "peace scares," when prospects for arms agreements have brightened, and has risen on news of enlarged military programs. Indeed, the growth industries, those whose profits have increased the fastest since 1929, are those most intimately bound up with defense spending.

This global approach to arms spending, however, obscures the sharp differences within the economy. The degree of dependence on arms varies enormously from General Dynamics to General Foods, from San Diego to Sarasota, from an electronics technician to a washing machine salesman. Moreover, even if the salesman, Sarasota and General Foods gained what the technician, San Diego and General Dynamics lost from disarmament, it is not at all certain that the end result would be a standoff. Jeremy Bentham shrewdly observed that the pain caused by the loss of income outweighed the pleasure resulting from an equal gain. Thus, the pain of disarmament should be studied in some detail.

The fortunes and jobs of three principal industries are closely bound up with arms outlays. About 95 percent of the employment in aircraft and missiles, 60 percent in ships and boat building and 40 percent in radio and communications equipment depends on defense orders. By 1965, more than

1,750,000 workers in these three industries alone will be tied
to arms spending. In contrast, for example, only about 2 percent of the construction industry's output and 80,000 of its
workers are absorbed by military outlays.

The range between localities and states is just as wide. In
1959, aircraft and missile production alone accounted for four
of five manufacturing jobs in San Diego, nearly three of four
in Wichita, one of two in Seattle and one in four in the Los
Angeles–Long Beach area. In 1960, the payrolls of four leading arms industries and the federal defense establishment
poured $4.3 billion into California, 10 percent of the state's
personal income; Texas collected $1.3 billion or 7 percent of
its personal income from the same sources; New York, $1.3
billion and 3 percent and Virginia $1.1 billion and 15 percent.
In states like Alaska and Hawaii, government defense agencies
and the four industries accounted for more than one of every
five wage and salary dollars. For the nation as a whole, 5 percent or $21.2 billion flowed from these reservoirs.

The dollar figures tend to understate the economy's dependence on arms. When the Boeing plant in Wichita loses
orders, its workers are not the only ones to feel the pinch. As
they cut their spending, grocery stores, home builders, appli-
ance dealers and car salesmen all lose business. These firms in
turn lay off workers whose spending is reduced and so on in an
ever-broadening ripple effect. This is the multiplier concept of
economics, a two-edged sword that raises all incomes by some
multiple of a fresh amount of spending and similarly lowers
incomes by a multiple of a given cut in spending. The multiplier for arms outlays has been estimated at between 2 and
2.4. In other words, removal of the $56 billion in arms outlays
would shrink total demand by $112 to $134 billion. This is a
range of one-fifth to nearly one-fourth of the nation's total
output.

If the sudden stoppage of arms orders would bring deep depression to the nation, it could spell catastrophe for Wichita and California. But nothing like this is within the realm of probability. Apart from any domestic pressures, the world powers themselves contemplate at most only a gradual and partial elimination of arms spending. However, the stark arithmetic of the extreme case underlines the economy's stake in war spending.

There is nothing new in this. It did not begin with the Cold War. The economy's link to weapons was forged nearly a quarter of a century ago. The plain fact is that the New Deal did not end the nation's massive unemployment; World War II did it. Between 1933 and 1939, the rate of unemployment in any single year never dropped below 14 percent and at least 7.7 million men were out of work. In 1939, the year before the defense buildup began, arms outlays were only 1.5 percent of the nation's total spending and there were 9.5 million jobless. Five years later, the war was absorbing 45 percent of our spending and unemployment had been wiped out. The jobless rate was an uncomfortably tight 1.2 percent. "Still greater prosperity could have been achieved by other means," Hitch and McKean have said. "But as a practical matter, the other means were not found or applied."

The remarkably successful conversion from war to peace is the principal source of the simple belief that disarmament now would bring no economic problems. The Soviet Union cited this in support of its optimistic reply to the United Nations inquiry. At a first and superficial glance, the evidence appears overwhelming. Between 1945 and 1947, military outlays were slashed by more than $120 billion in dollars of 1959 purchasing power, nearly as much as all the arms spending around the world today. From nearly 40 percent of the nation's total outlay, arms spending dropped to 5 percent. But the unemployment rate rose very little, from a cramping 1.9 percent to 3.6 percent. This new level was even better than the vanishing goal of 4 percent that the Kennedy administration had established as its high employment target.

History, however, cannot repeat itself. When peace came in 1945, the economy was vastly different from the one we live in now. In the happy phrase of A. S. Goldberger, the nation then had "a hope chest of suppressed desires—and a treasure chest of accumulated funds—which had filled up during the war years." With rising incomes and fewer goods on which to spend them, consumers had piled up $160 billion of savings during the war. The $255 billion of wartime deficits rolled up by the government became surpluses for goods-starved individuals. By 1944, consumers were saving more than one dollar of every four they earned. After the war, this backlog of effective demand was turned loose on cars, refrigerators, homes, clothing, phonographs, television sets, vacations, schools, roads and all the other goods and services that were rationed or nonexistent during the war. By 1947, consumers were saving less than three of every hundred dollars they earned. Their great outpouring filled much of the gap left by the withdrawal of the government from the marketplace.

At the same time, a happy combination of public and private decisions kept the economy buoyant and unemployment low. Many women and older men, drawn into the work force by the war's demand and high wages, went back to their homes. In a year and a half, the armed forces mustered out more than 10 million men, but great numbers took advantage of the GI Bill to go to school instead of flooding the job market. With the relaxed pace of peace, overtime hours were reduced in many plants. On the positive side, total demand was bolstered by a variety of government policies. Taxes were cut; easy loans were extended to veterans for housing and farms; war contracts were broken off with generous settlements.

Moreover, few World War II companies were war babies exclusively. Unlike any of the specialized concerns born in the Cold War, most wartime plants had experience in civilian markets and could reconvert with relatively less pain. Now, however, the aerospace-nucleonics-electronics complex has become the nation's first substantial "permanent war industry," in the words of Professor Emile Benoit of Columbia. In addition after World War II, leading private companies planned in advance for reconversion. Under the aegis of the business-supported Committee for Economic Development, they mapped out their probable postwar markets and these plans encouraged them to make the investment necessary to satisfy the expected demand.

If the postwar experience is a poor parallel for the future, the post-Korean arms cutback is more in point. Between the middle of 1953 and the middle of 1954, arms spending was reduced by $11 billion. The economy promptly went into a minor tailspin, with unemployment climbing from 1.7 million to 3.7 million. However, the combination of a tax cut in 1954, deliberately low interest rates and plenty of credit plus a rapid buildup in consumer installment buying brought a rapid if brief recovery.

Flawed as it was, the Korean record could not be played again, either. Unlike prospective disarmament proposals, that was largely a once-and-for-all defense cut, concentrated in a single year. The nation did not then as it must now look forward to a succession of reductions for four, eight or twelve years. It is unlikely that consumers now would be as willing to add as much to their debt as they did in 1955, particularly in the face of high unemployment. Finally, there was a recession, however mild. In fact, the continuing slowdown in economic growth began around 1953.

Perhaps the most heartening feature of the Korean cutback is the present realization that the Eisenhower Administration did not regard it as a serious demobilization. That mistake need not be made again. Indeed, the official United States reply to the UN disarmament inquiry said, "It is now clear that fiscal and monetary policies might have been applied (after Korea) with more vigor."

The current economy's sensitivity to cutbacks in military spending was demonstrated again in mid-1957. That fall, the yearly rate of arms outlays was sliced about $1 billion. Orders placed for military hardware were slashed more sharply. President Eisenhower's Economic Report for 1959 listed both factors among the major reasons for the short, sharp recession of 1957–58.

Under President Kennedy, defense outlays rose steadily and no new test has been made.

On its face, this is a dispiriting record. It appears to reflect an economy heavily interwoven with military spending, unable to rely on post-World War II experience for a demobilization parallel and remarkably sensitive to fluctuations in arms outlays. But there is nothing inevitable or foreordained about any of this. If we cannot reproduce the conditions of the past, we need not repeat its errors.

Clearly, the cold war effort eats up an enormous quantity of muscle power, brain power and resources that could be employed in creating a more abundant life at home and abroad. There are enormous, unsatisfied desires to be filled and a quality and temper of civilization to be enriched in the United States. There is, as we have seen, a great reservoir of poverty and near-poverty at home. Even this is dwarfed by the material misery in most of the globe. The trick, of course, is to convert energy and resources devoted to arms to the production of peaceful goods and services.

There are four principal economic problems attached to conversion; and the word "economic" should be underlined. For all four problems, there are well known answers. This is why the UN's experts, capitalist and communist, from rich nations and poor, all concluded "that all the problems and difficulties of transition connected with disarmament could be met by appropriate national and international measures."

On the home scene, the first problem is supporting total demand, filling the gap in orders caused by a cutback in government arms outlays. Here the familiar fiscal and monetary measures of compensatory finance come into play. Some of the reduction in government spending could and should be met by reductions in taxes. With more cash in their pockets, taxpayers—individuals and businesses—would increase their spending for appliances, homes, paintings, night clubs, salesmen, vacations, engineers and new machines. However, if arms cuts were matched dollar for dollar by tax cuts, there would still be some decline in total demand. This is because some of the extra income would leak into savings and would not be spent.

For this reason alone, some of the offset should be in the form of increased spending on government civilian programs. Moreover, victims of rush hour traffic jams, parents with children in overcrowded schools and city dwellers trapped in slums and hungry for parks, are likely to agree with Professor Galbraith and others who argue that the quality of American life is deteriorating because public expenditures have been pinched. A menu of possible public programs to fill the arms slack is simple to compose. Some of the more obvious ones are slum clearance, school construction, enlarged water supply, conservation of natural resources, recreation, hospitals, a war on disease, air pollution, mass transportation and roads, an attack on poverty.

In 1960, the National Planning Association, a study group of businessmen, labor leaders and scholars, estimated the expenditures needed for a handful of government programs over five years. They calculated that $66 billion annually should be spent, but that federal, state and local governments were likely to spend only about $30 billion a year. The annual shortfall of $36 billion is four to seven times as much as a reasonable estimate of the annual cutback in a plausible disarmament program.

As a backstop to these fiscal measures of reduced taxes and increased spending, credit probably should be easy. The Federal Reserve would be expected to supply banks with enough reserves to keep borrowing costs low and satisfy borrowers' demands for funds.

The second problem stems from the fact that swords are simply not ploughshares. Even if total demand is maintained, a discharged missile base airman can't step into an opening for a highway engineer; a laid-off electronics technician isn't likely to join the expanding staff of an art gallery; General Dynamics is not well equipped to produce schools and North American Aviation has not had any experience designing subway systems. These are the structural problems that were solved with such remarkable ease after World War II and against a background of enormous private demand.

The postwar experience is heartening in this respect, however. It shows how remarkably flexible and adaptive the economy can be. On the other hand, the persistence of depressed pockets in coal mining, textile and other regions, even during boom years, shows that some structural problems require special techniques. Here again, however, there are some well-known approaches. For demobilized servicemen and laid-off workers, generous discharge payments and longer, bigger jobless benefits can ease the transition. Publicly financed retraining programs could better match some men to new jobs. Although congressmen don't like losing constituents, counterpressures might be developed for relocation allowances, helping workers to move where job openings exist. War plants might be given large payments to terminate contracts and inexpensive loans to carry them through conversion. A systematic effort to explore new, civilian markets could be made like the CED's wartime effort. Communities heavily dependent on arms orders could be assisted like those enrolled in the program to assist depressed areas. They might receive federal loans and grants to study how new plants could be attracted and to finance their erection on easy terms.

Like the support of over-all demand, the structural problems of reconversion can be solved with relatively little pain —on paper.

A subtler difficulty arises from the fact that so much of our search for new knowledge and new applications of knowledge are financed by arms spending. The heavy military outlays for research and development are an important influence on the nation's rate of economic growth. About half of the $14 billion spent on research and development in 1960 was paid from military programs. Since economic growth depends on new resources and more efficient ways of using those resources, research and development is a powerful engine for faster growth. From it flow the innovations that enable an economy to use fewer resources for a given output or combine a fixed amount of resources in new combinations that yield a much higher output. The civilian economy has earned some large dividends from research financed by the military. Industries as grandiose as electronic computers and as commonplace as precooked frozen foods trace their origins to military research. Benoit of Columbia concludes "that most of the important new products and processes appearing in the last decade seem to be the fruit of earlier defense-supported research." If there was nothing to take the place of the military's outlays for scientists, engineers, laboratories and equipment, the lagging growth rate could be further weighted down.

But once again, there is no shortage of worthwhile civilian projects to which these human and material resources could be applied. Some experts in this field think that civilian research and development have even been retarded by the military claims on these resources. Among the possibilities are: the new technology required for inspecting arms agreements; a civilian space program; faster development of atomic energy for civilian power; developing solar energy; exploiting ocean resources; a broader attack on disease; a full-scale inquiry into the technological barriers impeding the development of the world's poor nations. This last opens up an especially exciting area of inquiry. A panel advising the United States Arms Control and Disarmament Agency foresaw research and development tackling such problems as: development and mass production of teaching machines; solar engines; techniques for overcoming aridity and restoring desert areas; population control; large-scale production and transportation of essential nutritional elements that are lacking in tropical countries; techniques for using low-cost labor to mass-produce road-making materials and machinery, housing, farm equipment, power systems, machine tools and factories. Indeed, Benoit believes that "a large backlog of such contracts in the hands of our major defense contractors would do more than anything else imaginable to allay anxiety and reduce latent opposition to defense cutbacks."

So far, we have been considering the problems of disarmament in a domestic setting. But its effects would not be confined to this country. A reduction in arms spending would have important consequences for economies overseas, particularly those of underdeveloped nations. Many of these countries depend on the export of a single raw material for the bulk of their overseas earnings. And these earnings, even more than foreign aid, enable them to buy machinery, manufactured consumer goods and a wide array of other products that they don't as yet produce for themselves. The world's military machines are major customers for several of these commodities. For example, the UN experts calculated that military demand consumes more than 8 percent of the world's oil, about 15 percent of the copper and more than 9 percent of the nickel, tin, lead and zinc. If nothing replaced the military demand, prices of these commodities and the hard currencies they earn would fail sharply. The effect on the oil-producing Middle East and Venezuela or copper-producing Chile could be staggering. The UN consultants estimated that a mere 6 percent drop in the export prices of the primary producers would cancel out half of all the grants and loans they receive from wealthier nations each year.

Moreover, countries like South Vietnam, Korea, Nationalist China and Turkey receive massive injections of American military aid. As this is reduced, a major stream of dollar earnings would dry up. (At the same time, there would be one beneficial domestic byproduct; the deficit in the United States' balance of payments would shrink.)

Again, however, there is nothing inevitable about so grim a picture. If the reduced military spending was offset by an equal amount of increased private and public spending, the fall in world demand for commodity prices would be very small. Moreover, some of the resources freed by disarmament could be diverted to investment in the world's poor countries. Demobilized officers and engineers and scientists could contribute substantially to breaking down the barriers to development. The scientifically sophisticated weapons-making companies are fine candidates for exploring the frontiers of solar energy, mass teaching machines and the like.

If the wealthy, armed nations put one percent of their output into foreign aid—a small part of the eight to nine percent they now devote to arms—incomes of persons in the poor countries would rise three times as fast, the UN has estimated. Incomes per person in the backward sectors of the globe are now rising slowly, about one percent a year; if world foreign aid rose to $15 billion annually or one percent of the output in advanced countries, incomes of the poor would climb 3 percent a year.

All at once, the economic problems of disarmament seem to have evaporated. Indeed, instead of creating problems, disarmament appears to offer enormous opportunities. At home, resources could be devoted to purifying the noxious air of cities, wiping out slums and abolishing poverty; abroad, the dishearteningly slow advance in material well-being might be converted to a more inspiring pace. This is the vision that the UN experts hold out:

> In a disarmed world, a general improvement could be expected in the level of living, including an increase in leisure. With the end of the armaments race, governments would accord social objectives a higher priority. The psychological, moral and material evils of compulsory military service and of stationing troops away from their homes would be avoided; so would the danger that security considerations and the armed forces might play an extensive role in forming the values of the community. Scientific cooperation and the arts would benefit from an extension of international exchanges.

The words have an intoxicating ring, but their sound should not drown out the clamorous problems that remain. Solutions advanced on paper are not self-executing. There is no guarantee that the proper measures will be taken. In fact, there is plenty of evidence to suggest that they won't.

If disarmament is to prove a blessing and not an economic curse, it is clear that there must be advance planning for the transition. Almost every serious student of the problem, regardless of ideological predilection, has recognized as much. The planning envisaged here, it should be emphasized, is not the planning by fiat of statist regimes. It is rather the advance identification of the special problems and the outlining of fiscal blueprints and particular programs that policy makers have successfully employed in the past. Whether these tools can be strengthened by some form of noncoercive planning is discussed in the last chapter. The point is to spell out the problems and programs now, before disarming begins. Plans for tax cuts and the expansion of specific government undertakings, policies to deal with the structural, growth and overseas dilemmas should be worked on before arms spending is reduced. This will serve two purposes: help calm the fear of those who believe their future is imperiled by a cut in arms spending (and who thus remain a potent political obstacle to disarmament) and insure that appropriate measures to hurdle the difficult transition will be taken.

The official reply of the United States to the UN's disarmament questionnaire made the point explicit. In the colorless language of governments, the United States said: "Advance planning and sensible policies at all levels of government will be essential to the maintenance of over-all economic activity in the face of the progressive diminution of defense demand."

The panel advising the Arms Control Agency declared that disarmament "should create small danger of provoking immediate depression in our economy, assuming sensible adjustment policies and vigorous government leadership to dispel adverse effects on business and consumer anticipations and to provide reassurance that aggregate demand will not be allowed to decline precipitantly."

The panel concluded: "Advance planning by government at all levels and by business firms, labor unions and other private organizations is required if the economy is to adjust smoothly to significant changes in the level of defense spending, particularly such as would result from general and complete disarmament."

William McChesney Martin, the chairman of the Federal Reserve Board and a pillar of orthodox business thought, has testified that in the event of disarmament "public confidence in overall economic prospects must be preserved. It is of the utmost importance that the government be prepared to act quickly to meet any developments and that this determination be generally understood . . . Much as I believe in the market process and the desirability of private enterprise, I think that government would have to assume a role . . . [in] mobilizing our resources . . ."

What are the prospects for the adoption of "advance planning and sensible policies?" At this point in time, somewhat dubious. The chief obstacles to a successful conversion, the panel of the Arms Control Agency declared, are "political resistance rather than deficiencies in our economic knowledge."

The simple fact is that most business leaders, among others, are hostile to planning by government and opposed to an expansion of welfare and social spending. They regard both as a threat to their power, prestige and, to a lesser extent, their fortunes. Moreover, many of those corporate leaders who would like to see arms outlays reduced often talk of returning the proceeds to the private sector exclusively in the form of tax cuts or a reduced national debt.

If planning and welfare spending successfully solve problems of unemployment and improve the quality and quantity of material life, businessmen rightly fear that there will be less uncritical enthusiasm for private enterprise and increased support for a society in which the corporation's dominant role is diminished. Some businessmen regard welfare projects, particularly in fields like housing or power, as competitive with private enterprise. At the simplest level, as welfare outlays rise, taxes tend to be higher, leaving businessmen less to dispose of for themselves.

In contrast, arms spending poses few of these threats and scatters some obvious blessings. It does not compete with anything private concerns produce for civilian markets and it is a source of business. It does not appear to embody any threat to the power and prestige of business leaders and may enhance both. From a businessman's vantage point, the only drawback to military outlays is that they tend to keep up taxes.

While corporate leaders appear to have the strongest motives for resisting measures for a painless conversion, they are not the only group with an interest in arms expenditures. Some labor unions whose members are employed in defense industries have lobbied vigorously for bigger military budgets and protested strenuously over every cutback. Political and civic leaders in communities threatened with the loss of a base or a contract have fought to preserve arms dollars. Some cities and states continually complain in Congress and at the Pentagon that they are not getting their rightful share of the military outlays. Finally, the armed forces themselves, or at least their leaders, are the single most potent source of support for ever-increasing arms spending. The place of generals, admirals and would-be generals and admirals in a disarming world is obviously a painful prospect for many. Indeed, one of the most challenging tasks of any disarmament will be the retraining of military officers for new tasks at home and abroad that fruitfully exploit their managerial and administrative skills.

Given this array of forces, a well-worn routine has been played again and again on the postwar stage in Washington. New welfare measures meet massive opposition; increased arms spending is approved with relative ease and often great enthusiasm. President Kennedy defended his planned deficit in the 1963 budget message by promising to reduce nonmilitary spending. He did not hesitate, however, to call for another increase in arms outlays, this one of $2.6 billion. Many of the very congressmen who deplore the deficit and demand that expenditures be cut then vote quickly for bigger military expenditures than even the President proposed.

The point is that the orders, incomes, jobs, and profits now enjoyed by Boeing, Wichita, the generals and the members of the Machinists' union, are tangible birds in hand; the prospects of conversion to new tasks, new industries and new jobs are off in some dimly perceived bush. The pressure to keep and enlarge a known present clearly outweighs the attraction of an uncertain future.

Apart from these serious institutional obstacles is the complex of attitudes clustered around the national debt. It was the rise in the debt that created the surpluses for business and consumers to pay for the great increase in private spending after World War II. But this is not generally well understood. In a disarming world, there is likely to be considerable popular support for using the reduced government spending to pay off the debt. What would happen in this case? If banks and other institutions receive federal dollars for their government bonds, their ability to make loans would certainly rise. But the prospect of borrowers appearing to seek loans and maintain spending is dim. For, as we have seen, purchases or total demand would be shrinking by some multiple of the government's reduced spending. And business firms and consumers are not likely to go deeper into debt, to enlarge their plants or their buying in the face of shrinking demand. Thus, popular misconceptions about the role of the federal debt could be another formidable barrier to adopting the proper policies.

Finally, as Martin of the Federal Reserve noted, the success of conversion depends in great measure on business and consumer confidence. If firms and individuals believe that employment will remain high, that incomes will grow, they are much more likely to maintain or increase their own expenditures. But if they doubt that there will be offsets to arms spending, if they fear rising joblessness and diminishing demand, they will probably compound the difficulty by cutting down their own outlays.

The confidence question is complicated now by two factors. Unlike World War II and Korea, future disarmament will almost certainly not take place in one major cut. Instead, businessmen and consumers will have to face a succession of steady cuts over years. The Arms Control Agency panel, for example, took as a realistic model for its calculations a disarmament program staged over twelve years. This relentless succession of cuts could have an important dampening effect on confidence unless there was a widespread belief in the efficacy of offsetting programs.

Moreover, disarmament now would come to an economy that is in some straits. Growth is slow and unemployment is inching higher. During World War II and Korea, the economy made rapid strides and employment was overfull. The credibility of offsetting measures will be dampened unless the existing and deepening pools of jobless are dried up.

Finally, there is a deep-seated belief in American society generally and among businessmen in particular that planning is impossible in a free society. This scepticism not only weakens belief in the possibilities of appropriate offsets. It also reinforces opposition to the very policies needed to cope with a disarming economy. A General Electric executive, Richard C. Raymond, has expressed a characteristic industrial view on this score. In language more moderate than his peers usually employ, he said:

> A successful industrial conversion requires a myriad of individual choices on the part of all the people concerned. Experience has shown that many of these decisions will take unpredictable twists, even in a highly authoritarian, centrally controlled community. The complexity and unpredictability of the total situation suggests that no individual or small group can assume responsibility for planning the whole process in advance. To regulate all these decisions by the action of any of the groups of people involved poses many problems even

in a slave society. In an open society where competitive enterprise is valued as a key to progress, it is impossible. Each independent decision has an effect on all the others.

Ironically, Raymond's very title reflects the fact that there is already a great deal of planning in the economy. He is the manager of the Technical Military *Planning* (my emphasis) Operation of GE's Defense Systems Department. In other words, the most devoutly private of private enterprises plans. Indeed everyone, consumers and businessmen, engages in planning of sorts. A decision to buy a house or a car, enlarge a plant or build a new machine involves a plan, implicit or expressed. But Raymond is making a somewhat different point. As he remarks, a developed economy is a complex, interrelated affair in which a decision in steel, for example, affects decisions in coal, railroads, autos, among consumers, food growers, food processors and the like. In view of this complexity, can the government make meaningful calculations about the consequences of particular policies? Can anyone estimate, for example, what would happen to employment in the chemicals industry if an arms cut was offset by a given amount of extra spending on roads or schools?

The answer, within limits, is "yes." A remarkable tool of economic analysis, used all over the world in countries with widely different economic systems, has been invented to meet just such problems. This is the input-output technique devised by Wassily W. Leontief of Harvard. It deserves to rank with Keynes' idea of examining the economy as a whole and Gardiner Means' concept of corporate pricing in administered markets as one of the great achievements of modern economics.

Input-output analysis traces the complicated web of relationships between industries by computing the amount each takes from and gives to the other. Thus, the technique shows how much steel, aluminum, zinc, copper, textiles, yarn, glass, rubber and all the other inputs are required for a given amount of automobile and truck production. At the same time, it shows how much auto and truck transportation is required to produce given amounts of these industries' outputs.

Input-output accomplishes this by arranging the industries of an economy in a matrix or table of horizontal and vertical columns, much like the detailed grid of wins and losses for a baseball league. In the baseball standings, each team appears in both the horizontal and vertical columns because it has both won and lost against other teams. A Senators' fan, for example, reads the numbers in the horizontal column to discover how many games Washington has won from every other club in the league. As he reads down a vertical column, he discovers how many games Washington has lost to every other team. An input-output matrix lists every industry in both horizontal and vertical columns because each is both a producer for and a consumer of the products of other industries. As an economist reads off the numbers in the horizontal column, he discovers, for example, how much the textile industry sells directly and indirectly to every other industry. Reading the vertical column, he discovers how much the textile industry buys directly and indirectly from every other industry.

Once the complicated task of filling in the data for such a grid is completed, the input-output tool becomes a powerful instrument for determining the effects of increases or decreases in one industry or one sector on all the others.* The panel of the Arms Control Agency used a model of the economy designed by Leontief and Marvin Hoffenberg to calculate

---

* Of course, these relationships don't stay frozen. Yesterday's ton of steel may have required 1.9 tons of coal. Today, thanks to a new furnace or some substitute product, only 1.8 tons are needed. But the relationships shift slowly enough so that good approximations of the consequences of a particular change like disarmament can be obtained for considerable periods of time.

how jobs would be affected by hypothetical cuts in military spending.

The panel began by assuming that military spending would be cut $17 billion in the first three years of a disarmament program. It then assumed a further cut of $8.5 billion in the next three years and $13.5 billion more in the last six years. The experts then turned to the input-output model and computed that jobs in the chemical industry would shrink by 23,000 in the first stage, 15,000 in the second and so on; aircraft and missile employment would fall by 361,000 in the first stage, another 193,000 in the second stage and so on.

Leontief and Hoffenberg have gone a step further in a report published by *Scientific American.* They assumed that a 20 percent arms reduction would be matched by an equal amount of extra spending distributed proportionately throughout the economy. They then worked out rough calculations for the resulting increase and decrease in jobs industry by industry. All of this could be done on a much more elaborate and refined scale. With input-output, reasonably accurate measurements can be made showing how much in sales and how many jobs different industries would lose from different kinds of arms reductions. In the same way, estimates can be made of the increased business and gains in employment that would result from different kinds of offsetting measures. With such information in hand, programs to build schools, cut taxes, attack urban slums, retrain workers and the like could be designed with some degree of precision to fit economic as well as social needs.

But input-output analysis suggests planning, even if it is planning on paper and not the coercive planning of direct controls. Because of this, the technique has suffered a curious up and down existence in the federal government. After World War II, the Air Force became interested in input-output as a method of determining the strains and bottlenecks that would be caused by different levels of military spending. The service put up most of the money for a major project in this field. But not long after the Eisenhower administration took office, the new Deputy Secretary of Defense, Roger M. Kyes, killed the program. Kyes, a General Motors vice president, was apparently disturbed by the planning implications of input-output analysis. Other industrialists, including his boss, Charles E. Wilson, the Defense Secretary and former GM president, were alarmed for the same reason. Ironically, at the very moment that Kyes was wielding his axe, economists from GM and other large corporations were urging that the program be sustained. They recognized that the technique is ideologically neutral and could help industry make more surefooted investment plans. Towards the end of the Eisenhower era, an advisory committee to the Budget Bureau recommended that the input-output program be revived. As a result, the government has been constructing a new grid for the economy that will show the inter-industry relations of major producers. By making different assumptions about the pace of future economic growth, federal economists hope, among other things, to pinpoint more closely the employment problems of the 1960's.

This slice of history neatly illustrates two points. There are political and institutional obstacles to the needed policies and plans for disarmament. But some at least may be reduced by a more sophisticated understanding of where genuine self-interest lies. Indeed, the special case of disarmament is not without its relevance to the questions raised elsewhere in this book. The problems and solutions of a successful conversion are much like those involved in lagging growth and rising unemployment. Competition of the few, corporate non-responsibility and the absence of countervailing power pose roughly the same difficulties for an arming as a disarming economy.

8. Planning and Freedom:
A Modest Proposal

IN THE SIMPLER VERSIONS of the business creed, planning is an invention of the Devil. The word conjures up images of hard-eyed bureaucrats, commanding producers and choosing for consumers in a total state. The stereotyped belief holds that planning destroys private property and ploughs under the rights of man. Unlike a free market economy, a planned system is inefficient, clumsy and produces shoddy goods. Whatever its defects, a free market, decentralized economy, where private decision makers need consider only their own, self-defined interest, is the sole order consistent with higher living standards and personal freedom.

There is, however, growing recognition that this is a caricature, an inadequate description of both the contemporary condition and the real choices confronting societies. As we have seen, the free market economy is not nearly so free nor so decentralized as its more ingenuous celebrants assert. Just as important, new, noncoercive styles of planning have emerged in Europe, the very birthplace of individualism.

In the United States, giant corporations, disposing of vast resources, making crucial decisions about investment, employment and pricing, inevitably plan for themselves. The federal, state and local governments, producers of services on a vast scale and gluttonous consumers of both goods and services, necessarily plan too. These plans, corporate or government, may be called market research, projections or programming. The label is not important. The point is that decisions are not made instinctively or automatically but quite consciously and with forethought. For better or worse they are based on expectations about the future and made in the hope of shaping that future in some fashion.

To be sure, this kind of planning has a piecemeal, decentralized character that provides some nourishment for the traditional belief in an Adam Smith world. In Western Europe and Japan, however, a remarkable experiment has been conducted since the end of World War II that narrows the gap between theory and practice. Attempts are being made to integrate and make coherent the plans of the major economic decision makers. This new phenomenon, an unexpected triumph of gradualism, is a sophisticated synthesis of private enterprise and, in greater or less degree, democratic planning.

Since the reconstruction of their war-shattered economies, private businessmen in Scandinavia, the Low Countries, France, Italy, West Germany and Japan have enjoyed an almost uninterrupted prosperity that has confounded the less imaginative Marxist forecasts. Living standards have risen steadily for the mass of their people. Employment for most has been full and even overfull. Television, autos, traffic jams, economic security, smog and the other blessings and curses of a high consumption economy have become common features of the European landscape. Moreover, the new Europe and the new Japan have been built during the very decade when the American economy was struggling with rising unemployment and sluggish growth.

For the most part, this transformation abroad has taken place with little damage to individual initiative or personal freedom. Indeed, the boom and the new institutions that have grown up with it have apparently released energies that were previously untapped. If some Europeans are chafing over the intrusion of the state in their affairs, this discontent has not brought the better fed, better clothed and better housed burghers and workers to the barricades.

The new style of noncompulsory planning, the new techniques attempting to reconcile planning with freedom, have taken hold so deeply overseas that they are now regarded as irreversible. On a more modest scale, there is a parallel at home. Even Republicans in power found they had no stomach to chew up the complex web of federal intervention in economic affairs that the simplistic creed held to be private. This intervention, it should be recalled, involves setting minimum wages, providing old age pensions, regulating new stock issues, setting public utility and transportation rates, controlling deceptive advertising, compelling collective bargaining, determining the supply and thus the price of money, supporting farm prices, subsidizing or propping minerals prices, building highways and much, much more. Indeed, state intervention throughout the Western world has become so pervasive that Gunnar Myrdal of Sweden insists that the debate over a free or planned economy has led to "one of the least informed and least intelligent controversies of our time."

"As a matter of fact," says Myrdal, "ours is a rather closely regulated society, leaving a certain amount of free enterprise to move within a frame set by a fine-spun system of controls which are all ultimately under the authority of the democratic state."

In Europe, the new planning can be described as systematic confrontation of ends with means. In fact, confronting limited means with limitless ends is what economics is all about. But why do it systematically? The Dutch planners have suggested one answer.

"By making the discussions on important problems of social policy more rational," the Central Planning Bureau says, "a

contribution is thus made to the bridging of social controversies."

In Norway, the economist Ragnar Frisch contends that the
new planning is a bulwark for Western values. "If it is to be
at all possible to save the Western democracies," he writes,
"we must find a way to safeguard the freedom and ethical
and moral dignity of the individual in the true spirit of the
age of enlightenment and at the same time achieve full and
effective use of all resources, natural resources as well as human know-how."

This way has been found, he declares, through the new
planning.

At a less abstract level, hard-headed British businessmen,
worried over their economy's dim postwar performance,
pushed a Conservative government to adopt some of the new
continental technique. A cotton thread manufacturer from
Manchester, the spiritual home of individualist economics,
has said: "This is, of course, planning. But since all of us plan
in our own business, I see no reason why we should be afraid
of the word."

The new style of planning is so loose and so unlike the
totalitarian model that many American economists regard it
as an illusion or toy for their European counterparts. The
sceptics doubt that planning has had much if anything to do
with the boom in Europe and Japan. Inevitably, they cite
West Germany, one of the stars of the postwar economic
firmament, and a nation that has no visible planning apparatus. Invariably, they ignore the crucial role that the German
state plays in business investment and the opportunity this
has offered for quiet and persuasive coaching from the
sidelines.*

---

* *Business Week* estimates that the German government finances 55 percent
of all the nation's investment in plant, equipment and construction; owns more
that 70 percent of the aluminum and produces more than 40 percent of the

However, it would be absurd to single out the new planning as the sole cause of the European and Japanese prosperity. Indeed, the size of planning's contribution to the boom is difficult to measure. But even those economists most wedded to the Smithian image are convinced that planning has not hobbled progress. Stanislaw Wellisz of the University of Chicago, a citadel of classical economics, acknowledges in an otherwise critical estimate: "I am at least confident that planning did no harm to France." John Sheahan of Williams, whose preference for the classical order is explicit, concludes less grudgingly in his study of the postwar French economy: "Where market control exists, the next best thing to eliminating it is to bring the public interest to bear in industry decisions."

Sheahan has here touched on one reason for the enthusiasm with which the new planning has been adopted. It has the obvious virtue of leaving existing institutions largely intact. It seeks to improve their performance rather than uproot the structure. Economists understandably hunger to bring their models to life, to create a world of atomistic, competitive firms and atomistic, nonunionized workers all performing the intricate minuet composed by Adam Smith and his successors. Scholars of other disciplines, statesmen, politicians and plainer citizens have a greater (and perhaps more realistic) respect for the tenacity of institutions and a better understanding of the great forces that called them into being. The new style of planning takes the world pretty much as it finds it. It accepts the concentration of markets, dominated by a handful of firms, that characterizes most modern industry. It

---

autos, lead and zinc. In addition, the federal government has provided tax concessions and other subsidies to stimulate expansion in particular industries. By 1963, the government was forecasting prospects for development and laying out guidelines for labor and management. Clearly, reliance on the unimpeded play of the free market was something less than the official ideology would suggest.

sees a host of possible advantages, technological and political, that flow from this order. It accepts the existence of unions in the labor market and regards them as potentially fruitful organs of economic production and political expression.

The new philosophy of planning, however, suggests that these great institutions have no divine mandate to order their own affairs, and thus the affairs of society at large, without let or hindrance. Nor does it pretend that, left to themselves, they will behave just like the atomistic enterprises and workers of the classical world. Instead, the new planners say: let us, with a maximum of inducement and a minimum of coercion, through a diet more heavily laced with carrots than with sticks, harness the energies of these great institutions to socially desirable ends. These ends shall be determined by citizens generally, or, more accurately, their representatives.

The most striking characteristic of the new planning is its generally noncoercive nature. It is planning by assent. In contrast with the directed, compulsory planning of the communist world, the French call the new style, "indicative planning."

Indicative planning has received scant attention from American commentators, perhaps because most of them are wedded to the belief that planning and freedom are inevitably antithetical. But whether Europe and Japan have prospered because of or in spite of the new technique, their success should have compelled a closer look at the peculiar institutions they have developed.

In skeleton form, indicative planning follows this pattern. A group of government economists tentatively select a plausible rate of growth for their nation's economy. This rate, perhaps five percent a year, is based on two central elements: population forecasts of the probable growth in the labor force and the likely pace at which the productivity of these workers will increase at full employment. Then, combining past experience and possible future policies, the technicians draw up a model or projection of the economy's broad outlines four or five years in the future.

This model might spell out the likely shape of spending by households, by government and by industry. In trade-dependent Europe and Japan, it would include forecasts of imports and exports. The model gives a quantitive picture of consumption and investment, private and public. In other words, it is a projection of the broad sectors that make up national income accounts.

This statistical sketch of a possible future is then examined by key representatives of industry, labor, farmers and consumers and by officials from government agencies that make decisions affecting the economy. They accept, reject or modify the growth target; they criticize and adjust the projections for the broad sectors of the account. Once agreement is reached on this outline of the economy, on the great economic aggregates, it is translated into meaningful terms for individual industries and ministries.

In each major industry, leading businessmen, union executives, government officials and public representatives calculate the model's implications for their specific area of interest. This is not altogether remote from practice in the United States where, for example, executives of General Motors calculate the firm's investment, employment and raw materials needs on the basis of their private forecast of the economy's future shape. In Europe, however, industrialists—collaborating with other branches of society—estimate their industry's requirements on the basis of a common forecast.

The projections of the individual industries are then reconciled; bottlenecks are spotted; inconsistencies are, hopefully, eliminated. A new picture or model of the future economy is then drawn up. Government tax, trade, subsidy and other policies needed to achieve the targets are tentatively mapped out. The projection is given final shape by the nation's cabinet and sent to the legislature for debate. Here, a last look is taken at the projections that both predict and help determine the future division of the economic pie.

The legislators need not concern themselves with technical details (Has enough coal been provided for the expected level of steel production? How accurate is the projection for the number of youths entering the labor force?), but with larger issues of social policy. Does the model leave a big enough role for private enterprise? Should the public sector be enlarged? If so, should there be more or less emphasis on schooling, parks, roads?

The model is then adopted and becomes The Plan.

The plan does not embody orders, mandates or directives to private firms and to unions. Instead, the projection is a guide to their decisions and to those of the government. It is not a collection of piecemeal guides like those that large corporations and government agencies now draw up for themselves in the United States. It is a coherent, integrated projection on which the major groups in society have agreed.

Since it lacks sanctions, does an indicative plan make any difference? Is this merely an empty exercise in forecasting with no consequences? In Western Europe and Japan the answer is clear. There is general agreement that planning exerts an important and beneficial influence over the great decisions made by industry, unions and the government.

A look at some specific indicative plans will make clearer why this belief, an odd one by the standards of many American economists, has taken hold. Such an examination will also underscore some of the pitfalls in planning, demonstrate how far the actual techniques depart from our idealized sketch and perhaps offer some answers to America's economic and political dilemmas.

The best known version of planning by assent, the form most carefully studied by Britain, is the French. The logic of history suggests that planning should flourish in the country of Colbert, the seventeenth century finance minister who deliberately sought to encourage industry by state policy. Indeed, the promotion of industry has been a constant goal of the four modern postwar French plans. The construction of the fourth plan, for the years 1962 through 1965, shows how the method works.

The heart of the system is the Planning Commission, a small group of government economists, engineers and other technicians. This body was told by the government to draw up sketches of the economy for 1965 that would embrace several objectives. These included: full employment, balance in France's international accounts and a modest start on improving the quality of modern life. More specifically, this last goal meant shifting some resources from private consumer goods to public investment for an attack on noise and polluted air.

Aided by experts from the Ministry of Finance, the Commission outlined in early 1960 some alternative models. These assumed yearly rates of economic growth of 3 percent, 4.5 percent and 6 percent. The 6 percent model was discarded on the grounds that it would dangerously strain France's balance of foreign payments.

The alternative models were then discussed with the Economic and Social Council, a body representing the nation's principal interest groups. The Council urged a high rate of growth and recommended special emphasis on education, research, health and housing.

Armed with these reports, the government picked a 5 percent growth rate for the plan's tentative target. The Commission then drew up a more detailed sketch of the 1965 economy, projecting the probable levels of investment, consumption, imports, exports and other broad categories of the national income. It took one more step. Utilizing the input-output technique described in the last chapter, the Commission calculated how much each of about twenty principal industries would buy and sell from each other in an economy of the size forecast in the model. These estimates were made for mining, iron and steel, electricity, chemicals and the like.

Here, then, was a reasonably detailed blueprint of the possible shape of the French economy in 1965. Was it practical? Were reasonable estimates made of the required investment, employment and materials, of the likely output in each of the industries?

These questions were answered by the twenty-five Modernization Commissions. These bodies were dominated by industrial and financial leaders but they also include representatives of unions, farmers and other private groups. In the fourth plan, there was one Modernization Commission for each of twenty industries and five Commissions that cut across industry lines to deal with broad questions like labor skills and financing.

The Modernization Commissions made further refinements in the estimates. From their deliberations, too, came a new, overall growth target. The government was persuaded that 5.5 percent was more desirable than a 5 percent pace to insure full employment. However, the projections for each industry now did not mesh as neatly, one with another, as the more abstract blueprint drawn up earlier by the Planning Commission. So the chairmen of the Modernization Commissions and the planning officials met with each other to iron out the differences.

The Economic and Social Council was then called back into session to approve a final version. At last, the National Assembly—largely a rubber stamp in De Gaulle's Fifth Republic—was handed the plan for debate.

French officials like to stress that the Planning Commission and other government organs have no power to compel any firm to abide by the plan. The government can't allocate materials to cooperative companies and deny them to firms that balk. In a formal sense, nobody is bound by the blueprint. But the government is far from powerless in France or anywhere else in the modern world. Indeed, the French government's power to induce cooperation is much greater than the federal government's in the United States.

A significant portion of the French economy is owned and operated by the state. The government runs the gas, electricity, coal, communications and air and rail transportation industries. Important banks and insurance companies are nationalized. Government firms explore, develop and distribute oil; the Renault auto company is state-owned. If these enterprises alone adhere to the plan, they increase the prospect that it will be fulfilled.

In the private sector, the state exercises a powerful influence over investment. The government directly invests public funds in private enterprises; it invests indirectly by controlling the lending policies of the nationalized banks; and before any firm can float a sizeable issue of bonds, it must receive the government's consent. Only firms profitable enough to finance their expansion out of their own earnings can afford to disregard the suggestions and advice of the government.

(Ironically, the planners' very success is costing them control over private decisions. The French boom has swollen the profits of an increasing number of enterprises who were formerly dependent on government funds for investment. Now these firms finance their own way.)

In addition, the government has a battery of forces in reserve to compel cooperation. Price controls have been largely lifted since 1957, but the power to impose them remains. An industry's leaders could be persuaded to follow the plan through fear that otherwise controls over their products would be reimposed. The government can also dispense subsidies and tax privileges to encourage good behavior. In sum, the Planning Commission itself may not be able to order and direct but the government can exert much more than a hortatory influence over key private decisions.

But the question still remains: How effective has the plan been? There is no doubt about the French boom. The decade of the 1950's marked the fastest growth in the French economy in a century, a full 33 percent higher than the pace in the United States. In the past, French manufacturers typically practiced industrial Malthusianism, curbing investment and plant capacity to prop up prices, erecting cartelist and protectionist walls around firms. They have now been transformed into one of the world's most expansive and growth-minded business communities. Nevertheless, one distinguished scholar, Professor Charles Kindleberger of MIT, concludes that planning played little part in this, that "the basic change in the French economy is one of peoples and attitudes."

But what forces created the new men and the new attitudes? Kindleberger himself says: "French planning is in some important respects the opposite of planning. Knowledge of income and industry projections and faith in the inevitability of expansion are communicated to firms at intra- and inter-industry meetings. This is perhaps the most powerful effect and one which has a faint resemblance to a revivalist prayer meeting."

The faintly derisive tone of this estimate obscures one important strength of indicative planning. Collaborative forecasts, reinforced by the government's commitment to full employment and growth, encourage businessmen to believe that there will be an increasing demand for their products. Secure in the knowledge that key firms are acting on more or less the same assumptions of growth, convinced that the projections have a degree of realism and consistency that would not exist if each firm made its own separate projection, French businessmen have become much more willing to invest in expanded capacity and modern equipment. This willingness, supported by the state, tends to be self-justifying. For the very act of increased investment increases incomes and productivity, thereby creating faster growth.

This is not to say that French indicative planning is flawless. For one thing, the broad-based democratic direction implied in the idealized model has not been realized. The Modernization Commissions, for example, are heavily weighted with business and financial leaders; unions have a very modest share in the discussions. In the third plan, the French government enlisted nearly four management representatives for every labor member.

The businessmen taking part in these discussions would indeed be a transfigured breed if they did not draw up a plan that to some extent protected each participating firm and divided up market shares. Undoubtedly, planning aids the survival of some less efficient firms that would go under in pure competition. But neither in the United States nor anywhere else in the world does pure competition exist. The characteristic live-and-let-live competition of the few in America tends toward the same result as discussion among competitors. At the very least, under indicative planning the public interest conditions some of these private decisions.

There are some other dividends. The government's day-to-day economic policy making, whether broad-gauged fiscal and money policy or the narrower focus of a nationalized coal industry, is much more likely to be consistent. This is because government officials join with private decision makers, in selecting targets and making forecasts. In the United States, for example, the Federal Reserve System, dominating monetary policy, may be pursuing a deflationary course at the very moment when the Administration is pressing for higher employment and growth. With indicative planning, the French are less likely to run into this kind of paralyzing contradiction.

Finally, the technique offers a good vantage point for taking account of the quality as well as the quantity of economic life. This is reflected in the French decision to make a start, however hesitant, on expenditures for dealing with such industrial side effects as noise and air pollution.

Critics of planning often observe that targets are rarely hit on the nose, that the vagaries of human behavior, changes in technology and changes in prices yield results that the planners don't foresee. This is true but may not be nearly as important as the critics argue. It is probably more important to correctly calculate the direction of change, up or down. On this score, the French have done quite well. For example, the second plan for 1954 through 1957 projected increases of 25 percent for gross domestic output, 30 percent for industrial production and 28 percent for investment. The actual results were increases of 28 percent, 46 percent and 41 percent. In the third plan for 1958 through 1961, these three targets were undershot by a range of 3 percent to little more than 6 percent. Again, however, the direction of the change and its general magnitude were on target.

One point is clear; the peculiar mix of planning and private enterprise, of state stimulus and free decision making represents an abandonment of doctrinaire, either-or approaches in economic policy making. It is the kind of experiment that led the chairman of the steel industry's Modernization Commission to declare: "On n'est plus dans le pays de Descartes; on est plus près du pragmatisme des Anglais."

Still another variant of noncoercive planning is practiced in Norway. This nation's respect for civil liberties and history of stable governments makes it a more attractive political model than France. The Norwegian economy, however, is bound by much more extensive controls than the French, particularly over prices. Again, the government-owned sector is important with the state running public utilities, a big aluminum plant and a large electrochemical plant. The government has also used import curbs, construction licenses, special taxes and subsidies to allocate resources and implement plans. However, direct controls have been shrinking and final decision making is left largely in private hands.

In Norway, a National Budget Section makes yearly forecasts and groups of selected officials draw up longer term, four-year projections. These plans cover overall output, investment, consumption, imports and exports. Details for the economy's major sectors are filled in by particular ministries after consulting the business interests involved. The Budget Section then irons out inconsistencies. A cabinet committee reviews the plan and determines the major measures necessary to carry it out. The plan then goes to the Storting, the Norwegian parliament, for debate and guidance in future legislative actions.

At the end of 1962, the government moved to make the technique more systematic. The Storting approved a bill to create a permanent planning agency which would draw up the four-year projections and map out even longer range programs. The new scheme also provides for an economic council of government, industry and labor representatives to advise the planners.

Norway depends so heavily on trade that prices must be watched carefully to insure that the nation's exports will find markets. The government can control prices directly and exerts an important influence over costs by proposing guidelines for wage increases. However, bargaining is free at the top. Norway's employers and unions are grouped in two federations that strike a central agreement which is binding on the contracts of individual firms and unions. This degree of centralization, very different from the United States, probably makes it easier for guidelines to be effective. Although Norway has had some inflationary pressures, students of the economy conclude that the guidelines have been observed with considerable success. Two special factors have had a sobering influence here. Norway has had a Labor government supported by the unions, and the union leaders are well aware of the nation's dependence on trade.

Again, whether because of the plan or not, the Norwegian economy has performed well since the end of the war. Employment has been full, living standards and output have risen steadily, although not spectacularly, the goal of raising the income share earned by the poorest paid workers has been partly realized and inflationary pressures have not overwhelmed Norway's foreign reserves.

While Norway's economy has behaved well, by all odds the world's most spectacular postwar performer has been Japan. Between 1950 and 1962, Japan's total output more than doubled; that of the United States rose by only one half. During the 1950's, Japan's yearly growth rate was three times as fast as America's. Japan confidently looks forward to doubling her 1960 income in 1970. By then, the image of Japan as a nation where tens of millions eke out a marginal existence will be as obsolete as the samurai. There is every reason to believe that Japanese living standards at the end of the decade will be on the same level reached in prosperous Western Europe in the late 1950's.

Japan's loose-jointed version is perhaps the most indicative and least coercive of the planning techniques adopted in the postwar world. Indeed, the economy's actual performance has so far outrun the planners' forecasts that sceptics of planning's importance can argue Japan as their best case. An American commentator, Michael Sapir, speaks of the "aura of academic unrealism" surrounding plans that miss their targets by so wide a margin. For example, the targets for the five-year plan ending in 1962 were reached in 1960. So that blue print was scrapped for the new, ten-year income doubling scheme.

However, a distinguished Japanese economist, Miyohei

Shinohara, thinks these critics are missing a crucial point. Japanese firms, he observes, regard the plan forecasts as a "minimum line" below which they do not dare to fall. In order to hold on to their existing share of a market, Shinohara says, Japanese companies believe that they must make investments that exceed those called for in the plans. If they don't, they fear that they will lose out to their rivals. The plans then stimulate a kind of competitive, ever-expanding investment that in itself helps to enlarge incomes and demand.

Shinohara concludes: "This is a mechanism by which a reckless increase in investment is realized, and the extraordinary rate of growth is attained as a consequence. In this sense, one of the secrets of Japan's high rate of postwar growth may lie in the Economic Plans themselves, and in the sensitive responses of firm's investment behaviour to these Plans."

In Japan's conservative regime, the planning mechanism is even more heavily weighted on the business side than in France. The Japanese counterpart of the French Planning Commission and Norway's National Budget Section is the Economic Planning Agency. It is guided by an Economic Deliberation Council whose central unit includes industrialists, bankers and professors but not a single trade unionist, farmer or consumer representative. The Council has subcommittees for the economy's individual sectors and they are forged in the same business mold.

For the latest ten-year plan, through 1970, the planning agency and council drew up projections for the usual principal components of the economy. These were broken down for three broad industrial branches—primary industry like agriculture, secondary industry or manufacturing and tertiary industry like retailing. Growth targets for individual industries within these sectors were also forecast. The plan even attempts to project how workers will spend their income ten years off, although it is questionable how seriously this kind of detail is taken. Indeed, close students of Japanese planning complain that the forecasts are not really integrated, that each step is treated more or less independently of the others.

If Japan achieves the remarkable yearly growth target of 7.2 percent envisioned in the latest plan, clearly more than planning itself will be responsible. Japanese businessmen have a lot going for them. The most efficient Japanese manufacturers have some advantage in world markets because Japanese labor is paid much less than Western workers. (Although the actual trade advantage is not nearly so great as common belief holds. Japanese labor costs can be inflated by less productive workers. Moreover, Japan must import 90 percent of her raw materials and materials costs often outweigh labor costs in manufacturing.) In addition, the Japanese have been saving their incomes at a fantastic rate to finance investment. The fact that Japanese industry is concentrated has probably been another reason for the amassing of huge sums for investment. Shigeto Tsuru, another economist, thinks that much of the investment has been financed from high profits flowing from monopoly prices. Finally, Japanese manufacturers can also take advantage of the country's dual economy, the unique mix of advanced and primitive industries. This structure enables Japanese firms to buy parts or semifinished goods cheaply from the backward sector.

In fact, Japanese businessmen enjoy so many advantages, their role in the state is so dominant and the government has been so complaisant that Leon Hollerman has been led to conclude this about postwar Japanese planning: "It is the state which is being used to help achieve the goals of the private sector rather than the other way around."

Even so, the process has brought prosperity to the bottom as well as the top. Possibly because of Japan's feudal tradition of obligation and dependency or perhaps from a shrewd political sense that understands how to hold power, the business-dominated planners hold out some attractive inducements to the masses of people. The text of the "Doubling National Income Plan" is loaded with sentiments and proposals that might have been lifted from an old CIO convention.

For example, the document declares: "Full employment and higher living standard are the two ultimate ends for a modern State to accomplish." The plan envisions reductions in hours of work as well as increases in pay. It calls for both an absolute and a relative increase in public, social investment. Specifically, the plan says that spending for public housing, parks, sewage, transportation, conservation and water supply should rise from one third of the investment in private equipment to one half in 1970.

Housing can't be left to the private market, the businessmen-planners declare. Better housing "will serve not only to enhance the people's level of living but also to secure and reproduce labor power, ease social tension and expand effective demand." While the monopoly-minded businessmen urge the government to "save private industries from the damaging effect of excessive competition," they also call for increases in medical insurance and other forms of social security.

To be sure, much of this may be a verbal sugar coating for a business-designed pill. But if proposals like this, nominally endorsed by business and government, are repudiated, the mass of the people are not without recourse. In modern Japan, voters can punish at the polls those who deceive them. In any state with democratic pretensions, there is considerable political risk in failing to redeem *specific* pledges.

From this brief survey of the new planning in three very different nations, some common elements emerge. The new technique is an attempt to make rational collective choices about the future by confronting alternative claims on resources with a nation's probable ability to produce. By setting forth precise, quantitative goals or targets, the plans provide standards against which performance can be measured. This is useful not only to public and private economic decision makers but to an electorate. It enables voters to gain a more exact notion of how well its government has behaved in fostering—or failing to foster—material well-being.

The new technique permits large numbers of people to compare the costs against the benefits of alternative programs, to weigh the advantages, for example, of an expanded social security plan against its costs in private consumption. While the legislative debate over the plans has so far rarely lived up to its promise, the technique has important implications for democratic choice in the modern world. Conceivably, these debates could focus on a society's larger goals and the principal means for implementing them. This could relieve parliaments of the disability that frustrates the American Congress, excessive concentration on marginal detail and perfunctory attention to major ends.

The plans also provide one solution to the problem of legitimacy for economic decision making in an economy of concentrated economic power. They are conscious attempts to assert the public interest in important private decisions. But this assertion is not one-sided; it is not decreed. To a greater or less degree, the plans are drawn up by representatives of the major economic interest groups. These groups are not only involved in choosing the ways and means for broad national economic and social objectives. Within particular industries, they help set goals and discuss the roads to reach them. Unlike so many American conferences that bring together businessmen, union leaders, academics and other notables, the plan meetings are not platforms to repeat predetermined positions or hot houses for breeding platitudinous agreements. They are convened to make decisions about specific, measurable tasks.

In all these plans, the state can invoke some strong sanctions to encourage adherence. But greater reliance is placed on lures such as subsidies, investment funds and tax benefits. At bottom, however, the plans rest on the individual decisions of private decision makers. The plans assume that a plausible prospect, mutually agreed upon, will induce a fresh element of rationality into the actions of those who wield economic power.

As Prof. Sheahan has said, speaking of France, the task of the new planning is to provide a "system of information and promotion." This "falls well short of the view that it should provide active direction of the economy. . . . Information and promotion do not require that individual economic units conform to any coordinated plan." The system then preserves a large measure of individual choice and limits the extension of the central state.

How much of this technique can be exported to the United States? Has it any bearing on our own economic problems of the non-affluent two-fifths, lagging growth and high unemployment? Is it relevant for the domestic political problem of economic legitimacy? Clearly, these systems could not be transplanted intact. The American political economy is a very different animal from those we have examined.

In all three planning nations, the government is involved in the economy much more deeply than in the United States. Abroad, the state not only operates an important sector of the economy, it has a much stronger voice in allocating funds for investment by private firms. All three economies, too, are marked by more direct controls than the United States possesses or perhaps wants.

The political milieu in which business operates is very different, too. France and Japan have a tradition of overt, state-encouraged collaboration between potential competitors. In the United States, concentration tends to promote implicit collusion and erodes competition in price. But a live-and-let-live arrangement that can be upset by antitrust laws, by new firms or the revolt of an established company is not the same as open, state-promoted sharing of markets.

In both France and Japan, too, government and business have a history of active partnership. In Norway, the collaboration tends to run between the labor government and the trade unions and there is a greater degree of labor-management centralization than in the United States. At home, government policy may, as it has under Kennedy, reflect corporate aspirations but there is still a deep reservoir of mistrust by businessmen toward the government.

All of the planners are much more dependent on imports and exports than the United States. This cuts two ways. It places a stronger premium on planning but it makes forecasting more difficult because there are so many forces outside the planning nation's control. Imports amount to more than 40 percent of Norway's total output and Japan must import virtually all her raw materials. In France, foreign competition has been deliberately used as a spur to modernize backward plants. Despite the American preoccupation with the balance of payments deficit, imports here are less than five percent of total output.

Planning abroad was given great impetus by World War II. Much of the capital stock—plants and equipment—of Norway and Japan were destroyed by the war. Recovery could simply not be left to the blind dictates of private markets. The rapid defeat of the French armies by Nazi Germany probably drove home, among other lessons, an understanding that the unprogressive French industrial complex had to be modernized. The war had other consequences, too. In Norway, for example, German occupation induced a spirit of cooperation between labor and management. The exiled Norwegian government succeeded in bringing union and industrial leaders together on a postwar wage policy as early as 1944. The unoccupied, unbombed United States received no postwar legacies like these.

Finally, all three nations have an economic structure that is simpler than that of the United States. Their populations too are composed of fewer strands and this greater homogeneity may make indicative planning easier to undertake.

But a simple recital of these differences can exaggerate the gap between the American and the planning nations. There is already a great deal of planning in the United States, both long- and short-term, although it is on a piecemeal, uncoordinated basis. Apart from the projections that large corporations now make on their own, there is a wide range of government planning. Perhaps the most striking is the Federal Reserve's control over the volume of money. The System tries to adjust the supply of money or bank credit to the immediate needs of business and also to satisfy longer-term goals like a stable price level. Through its sales and purchases of government bonds from banks and through its control over the required level of bank reserves, the System daily fixes the power of banks to lend. This gives it a decisive influence over interest rates or the price of money. In effect, the System determines one half, the supply side, of the supply and demand equation that fixes the price of money. In agriculture, a complicated network of programs have been erected to influence the supply and price of many commodities. Similarly in oil, federal and state agencies collaborate to tailor the production of oil to demand at a given price.

Many industries have received federal subsidies in order to maintain a given supply of a product or support a particular price. Subsidies are or have been given to shipping, airlines, zinc, lead, copper and other stockpiled metals and materials. Prices or rates are determined by some unit of government for railroads, trucks, airlines, electric power, oil and gas pipelines among others.

Alongside of this piecemeal governmental planning, a network of collaboration between interest groups is slowly growing. There is as we have seen in most concentrated industries a tendency to escape competition in price and seek more secure arrangements, either legally and tacitly or illegally and explicitly. On the labor-management front, the tendency for countervailing to become coalescing power has already been discussed. Planning of another sort is also beginning to appear. A remarkable new agreement between the Kaiser Steel Corp. and the United Steelworkers provides a long-term formula for sharing productivity gains between workers and the company. In several industries—notably meatpacking, some railroad lines and the West Coast longshore industry—imaginative contracts have been signed that encourage modernization and protect workers against losing incomes because of technological displacement. In one sense, all collective bargaining agreements, with their elaborate provisions governing the work conditions and pay of industrial life, providing pensions, medical insurance, and rules for promotion, hiring and firing are instances of collaborative planning.

In sum, the conversion of this piecemeal planning into a coordinated scheme need not strain our institutional structure nor undermine the high value Americans rightly place on individual choice.

What shape would indicative planning take in the United States? It could begin with the President's Council of Economic Advisers. They already make annual projections of the economy's principal components for the government's internal use. These could be incorporated in a set of alternative projections for, say, five years into the future.

These calculations should be assessed by government agencies with economic responsibilities, by officials from the Treasury, Departments of Defense, Labor, Agriculture, Commerce and State, from the Federal Reserve Board and, perhaps, the key regulatory agencies. Indeed, officials from these agencies now scrutinize sections of the annual Economic Report that the Council prepares for the President. In a scheme of indicative planning, they would collaborate in determining precise, quantitative targets.

With such an arrangement, the likelihood of contradictory federal policies could be sharply reduced. Thus, if balance of payments deficits were regarded as a central problem, Treasury tax policies to curb overseas investment would get greater support and the Interstate Commerce Commission would be more likely to encourage cheaper, more efficient transportation. If agreement was reached, for example, on attaining a five percent yearly growth rate, the Federal Reserve Board would have to consider providing adequate supplies of money to sustain this goal as well as maintaining a steady level of prices. Just this kind of coordination was foreseen in Britain by *The Economist*. The paper predicted that planning would compel the British Treasury to think of expansion as well as its habitual worry about stability. "There is now a body of liberal outside experts," the weekly said, "whose function is to put ants in those [Treasury] pants."

Planning, of course, would not be left exclusively to technocrats and government officials. Key industrialists from steel, mining, electrical machinery, autos, oil, electric power, electronics, construction, retailing, banking and other major sectors should be brought in to examine the five-year model and revise it. They could be encouraged to translate its broad aggregates into specific levels of output, investment and employment for their own industries and firms.

Out of this process of integrated market surveys could come a greater degree of certainty. The risk that businessmen seek to avoid in so many areas would be reduced. Investment forecasts would stand a better chance of being realized if the key decision makers knew that all important firms were proceeding, along with the government, on the same approximate assumptions.

The technique could also yield industrialists some other dividends. Technical, material and labor shortages could be spotted in advance and plans made to overcome them. Managerial and technological knowledge could be more widely diffused. Unneeded plant capacity would be less likely to be installed and the prospects of putting in place needed investment would be enhanced.

For its part, the government could secure greater understanding and support for its own policies and programs. Businessmen might be less inclined to oppose legislation that met social needs if they saw how it fitted into and supported a model of future growing incomes. They might be more willing to follow pricing guideposts that they themselves helped to erect. The blessings of stable prices are obvious to those who lend money, live on fixed incomes or worry about deficits in international accounts. Less obvious is the fact that the success of any administration's expansion policy rests on business cooperation. Recall that the demand-creating powers of President Kennedy's tax cut, for example, could be wiped out if industry pushes up prices at the first sign of a quickening economy.

Unions, too, should be strongly represented in these mixed public-private consultations. In their absence, the temptation to expand economic output at the expense of workers might be irresistible. Moreover, if unions knew that business and government leaders were committed to specific and realistic programs of full employment and higher living standards, they could afford a longer view. Labor leaders would be much more likely to encourage support of wage guidelines and promote rather than resist technological change. In the present state of affairs, a union leader properly asks: "What's in it for me and mine if I try to hold back wage demands?" A genuine pledge of jobs for all who want work and systematic programs to achieve this could lead to different questions and bring different replies.

Delegates of other groups, farmers, consumers and academic experts should also play a role in indicative planning. The public representatives as well as the unions might speak for the unrepresented, unemployed and nonaffluent who would then have some prospect of winning a larger share of a growing national pie. Almost as important, these public spokesmen could introduce into the models some consideration for the quality of modern life. They might be the source of a new emphasis on enlarged recreational facilities, the destruction of urban blight and the creation of quieter, cleaner, greener cities.

Given the congressional intoxication with peripheral detail, it may strain the imagination to picture Congress, aided by the Joint Economic Committee and other committees, debating an appropriate growth rate, the mix between public and private expenditures, a choice between expanded social security and lower taxes for consumers. But many congressmen are concerned about the declining power of the legislature. The opportunity for an enhanced role, for a thoughtful examination of major questions, would be an attractive prospect to some legislators.

How much power the government should have to implement the plan—what taxes, subsidies and other legislation should be enacted—would be matters for the executive and the consulting bodies to recommend and for Congress to decide. But the principle of voluntary choice could and should be maintained. Companies and unions would be as free as they are now to make their own decisions. Even without legislation specifically designed to encourage adherence to the plans, self-interest would tend to encourage them to follow the paths laid down in the model.

Finally, indicative planning could fill another major need in a nation that periodically gropes for a definition of its national purpose. This point was perceived by Sir Robert Shone, the head of the new British planning agency, the National Economic Development Council. He has said:

"It would seem a major benefit of the French system that it faces all sections of the community with the problems of a common national objective, and an objective sufficiently inspiring to hold out the chance of securing co-operative effort in the achievement of stated goals."

Sir Robert's vision need not obscure some genuine problems in indicative planning, problems that have already been underscored by the French and Japanese models. Even the most forward-looking of private and public planners will necessarily be biased in favor of an existing industrial structure. Cold quantitative logic might, for example, lead to a conclusion that some steel companies are so poorly run that they should be allowed to disappear. But if executives from those firms take part in the planning process, it is expecting too much to think that they will assent to their own demise. There is, in other words, a tendency in indicative planning to keep large, inefficient firms in existence beyond the life they might expect under pure competition. Similarly, there is a great temptation to set output and investment targets within an industry that protect existing market shares. This in turn could dampen incentives to innovate, to make daring experiments that use resources more effectively.

But even in the absence of indicative planning, there are strong forces at work shoring up the status quo. These criticisms against planning are launched on the assumption of perfect competition. The fact is that competition is most imperfect, that concentration is the hallmark of most American industries. Under these conditions, corporate executives tend to play it safe anyway. They tend to make price and output decisions that satisfy all their 'competitors' and an implicit live-and-let-live policy is the rule.

A greater danger is that the planning mechanism will be

captured by the corporate executives, that the business voice will dominate the chorus of public and private planners. In Japan, industrial dominance over the mechanism is obvious. In France, Professor Sheahan concludes that the Planning Commission has more and more adopted the position of financial and manufacturing executives. The Commission, he says, has softened its early stress on structural reform within industries and has consistently backed higher profits, smaller wage increases, lower taxes, mergers and abolition of price controls. The Commission, he notes, gives "singularly little attention to questions of income distribution." Its departures from a conventional business line have been its emphasis on public investment in housing, education and social services and its forceful advocacy of full employment and expansion.

But the unplanned American society is subject to the same danger. Earlier chapters have traced the dominant role of the large corporations. Except in periods of great crisis, there is a tendency for business values to triumph anyway in both public and private policy. At the very least, indicative planning holds out the hope that the quality of these policies will be improved, that the concentrated corporations will set target rates of return in the expectation of expanding rather than fixed levels of output and employment.

Moreover, the planning technique is set in a framework in which the public voice can be asserted over investment, pricing and other economic policies. This arrangement may have more formal than substantive reality. But indicative planning does offer some potential for saturating an essentially authoritarian industrial structure with democratic processes.

Although many academics and virtually all corporate leaders denounce public planning with a fury that earlier ages reserved for sin, the United States has not been immune to the infection that has spread through Western Europe and Japan. In an embryonic, heavily disguised form, elements of noncoercive planning have already appeared on the American scene. The best known is the Employment Act of 1946. This pioneering piece of legislation commits the government to the promotion of high levels of employment and purchasing power. It is a nonenforceable verbal formula. But like all political pledges, it is not without its effect. It makes clear that the state is not to be an idle or passive actor in the economic drama. It says that the government has a role to play in sustaining and increasing material welfare.

The Employment Act implies that private markets cannot be expected to provide by themselves the increases in well-being that are within reach for all. The act further suggests that government is responsible for filling the gap, for redressing the shortfalls. In recent years, the act may have been more honored in the breach than in the observance. But the point is that it remains on the books. Neither the conservative Eisenhower nor the conservative Kennedy administrations ever thought of repealing it. As long as it exists, the act is a kind of silent reproach to the government for failing to fulfill the pledge. Like the more precise targets of indicative planning, it provides a gauge against which the economic performance of the party in power can be measured.

Moreover, the Kennedy administration took several more cautious steps in the same direction, even if their symbolic importance outweighed their substance. One was the creation under the leadership of the former Labor Secretary, Arthur J. Goldberg, of the President's Advisory Committee on Labor-Management Policy. This group of union, industrial, public and government leaders met from time to time to discuss and report on a wide assortment of problems like automation, unemployment and foreign trade. Its quadripartite structure is a remote cousin of the bodies that advise the European technocrats on indicative planning. To be sure, the resemblance should not be overstressed. The Labor-Management Committee largely included second echelon business leaders; the top tier would probably not cooperate. Moreover, the Committee was unable to agree on more than sweeping, generalized statements. And even these were sometimes constructed only after bitter disputes that threatened the experiment's precarious life.

What would happen if a stronger committee that included higher ranking industrial and financial hierarchs was given a more specific task? Would it perform better if it was mandated to advise on precise goals and targets like an attainable growth rate and the broad components of future national income?

For now, it is unlikely that stronger figures from the corporate elite could be recruited for such a task. But at some future time they might. Then the very nature of their job would prevent them from producing the ritualistic statements that have flowed from the Labor-Management Committee.

In the fall of 1961, President Kennedy's Council of Economic Advisers tried a tentative move towards noncoercive planning. The Council drew up what it called a "decisional model" of a full employment economy for 1963. The model projected the levels of total output, personal consumption, government spending, private investment, agricultural and manufacturing output that the Council thought would be needed to achieve an unemployment rate of four percent. The projections were sent to government officials, union presidents, private foundations and economists from the universities and leading corporations for comment. Among other things, the business economists were asked to translate their own national high employment projections into estimates for their particular industries. They were asked how full employment would affect the demand for their products, the investment they would need to make and the labor they would have to hire.

The experiment failed. The business economists declared a virtual strike. Among other things, they didn't want to be associated with a forecast that would necessarily show an extraordinary increase in profits. They were fearful of rousing union demands. Moreover, it is likely that the business aides regarded the invitation as a step towards more general planning. And this is still anathema in the corporate creed. They agreed only to forecast their own future output on the basis of a Council estimate of growth. And the business economists emphasized that they were not endorsing the growth estimate, that it was the Council's exclusively.

Despite this inauspicious start, the growing disparity between the performance of the American and the other capitalist economies is likely to increase the pressure for change. President Kennedy, perhaps a step ahead of the business community, asked his advisers in 1962 to give him a special report on the successful French economy.

Also within the government, we have seen that input-output analysis has been revived. A group of officials from several agencies is supervising a project that will use the technique to build models of the economy in 1970. These models will inevitably find their way into corporate as well as government policy making. Would the business creed be seriously impaired if business economists took part in revising the models?

Apart from the potential gains in material well-being, indicative planning holds some promise of solving a major political problem in modern economies, the problem of legitimacy. The lack of sanction for private, nonresponsible power troubles businessmen as well as other thoughtful citizens. The doctrine of corporate responsibility, it will be recalled, was invented precisely to supply this need. The doctrine has proven to be empty. But a technique in which general and particular publics participate in economic policy making could satisfy a hunger that meaningless fictions only frustrate. Finally, as Sir Robert Shone has suggested, noncoercive planning could be the means through which a fruitful search for national purposes is undertaken, a search that is not conducted ad hoc by an elite panel but a continuing process that engages the energies of many persons from many groups.

Clearly, indicative planning is no cure-all. It does not automatically assure access to a promised land where milk, honey, television sets, parks and culture overflow in abundance and the dignity and brotherhood of man are guaranteed. Indeed, like any institutional change it creates some new problems as it solves some old ones. Moreover, there is no need, particularly in a society that likes to regard itself as pragmatic or experimental, to rely on one device. As the nation moves toward the new planning, it could and should adopt some of the other proposals advanced in Chapter 3. An amended antitrust law to break up inefficient, Malthusian corporations would serve as an excellent check on the tendency of business planners to preserve their own. A wage-price hearing panel for corporate giants in key industries could reinforce the policies laid out by the planners.

In private or public life, planning is simply foresight, an extension of man's power to reason. It assumes that man is not a helpless creature of his natural or social environment but has some control over his fate. In an earlier age, when the forces of nature seemed overwhelming, when life for most was a series of numbing catastrophes, myths, demons, and incantations were necessary to rationalize a terrifying state of affairs. But technology has now put within our grasp the prospect of material wellbeing for all. If we cling to the rationalizing stereotypes that were appropriate for the economies of scarcity, if we hold to the obsolete claims for prestige and power of a narrow visioned few, the comfortable three-fifths of the affluent society may well continue to enjoy what they have. But the nation will then run great risk not only of being overtaken in a material sense by economies of East and West, but also of losing its pride of place as an innovator of the institutions that set men free.

Notes and Index

Notes

Chapter 1: The Corporate Vision and the New Frontier

page

1 Epigraph: Remarks of President Kennedy, Commencement Exercises, Yale University, June 11, 1962.

2–3 Hodges and BAC: Press conference, Feb. 14, 1961; *Washington Post*, Feb. 15, March 29, April 5, 1961.

3–4 BAC: Hobart Rowen, "America's Most Powerful Private Club," *Harper's*, Sept. 1960; Carl Reiser, "Luther Hodges Wants to Be Friends," *Fortune*, Aug. 1961.

4 Hodges accused by Textile Workers: *New York Times*, March 14, 1959.

4 Kennedy shown conservative: Reiser, "Luther Hodges."

5 BAC becomes BC: Blough to Kennedy, July 5, 1961; White House press release, July 10, 1961. Kennedy invites study: R. M. Blough, "My Side of the Steel Price Story," *Look*, Jan. 29, 1963.

6 Adviser on Kennedy: Conversation with author, 1961.

7 Kennedy anti-slump measures, directive to federal agencies: *Economic Report of the President*, Jan. 1962, p. 97 ff.
Interest rates: *ibid.*, pp. 86 ff.

8 Social measures: *Congressional Quarterly*, 87 Cong., 1 Sess. (1961), vol. XVII, pp. 247 ff.; *Econ. Report*, 1962, p. 102.
Similar Eisenhower measures: *Econ. Report*, 1959, pp. 33–43; Wilfred Lewis, Jr., *Federal Fiscal Policy in the Postwar Recessions* (Washington, 1962), pp. 221, 236 ff.

9 Hal B. Lary, *Problems of the United States as World Trader and Banker* (New York, 1963), pp. 83, 51.

10 Balance of trade: *Survey of Current Business*, U.S. Commerce Dept., March 1963, p. 19.

11 Gold supply: *Federal Reserve Bulletin*, April 1963, p. 493.

12 Kennedy, Message to Congress, Feb. 6, 1961; *Econ. Report*, 1962, pp. 10, 86–90.

13 Europeans: *Economic Surveys by the O.E.C.D.–United States–1962*, Organization for Economic Cooperation and Development (Paris, 1962). Securities Tax: Kennedy Message to Congress, July 18, 1963.

page
13–14 Trade Expansion Act: *Washington Post,* Feb. 14, 1962.
16 Eisenhower and wages: *Collective Bargaining in the Basic Steel Industry,*
     U.S. Dept. of Labor (1961), p. 150.
     Guideposts: *Econ. Report,* 1962, pp. 185–96.
17 "Our focus": Conversation with author, see *Washington Post,* April 29,
     1962.
18 President's letter: *Econ. Report,* 1962, p. 182.
18–20 Steel crisis, general description: Grant McConnell, *Steel and the
     Presidency—1962* (New York, 1963).
19 President's interview: *Washington Post,* Dec. 18, 1962.
19–21 Steel's viewpoint: Blough, "Steel Price Story."
     McConnell, *Steel,* p. 104.
21 Kefauver's study of steel: Bernard D. Nossiter, "Shadow and Substance
     on the New Frontier," *The Progressive,* Jan. 1963.
22 1963 steel price rise: *New York Times* and *Business Week* for April 20,
     1963. Archibald Cox, "Wages, Prices, Government and Lawyers,"
     Harvard Law School Bulletin, June 1962.

Chapter 2: Blue Chips and Tax Carrots

24–26 Business organizations seek three changes: (1) Donald J. Harden-
     brook, "What Ought to Be Done," press release from Natl. Assn. of
     Manufacturers, Oct. 5, 1962; (2) *Reducing Tax Rates for Production
     and Growth,* Committee for Economic Development (New York, Dec.
     1962), pp. 28–29; (3) *The Right Kind of Tax Cut at the Right Time,*
     Testimony before the House Ways and Means Committee, March 18,
     1963, U.S. Chamber of Commerce (Washington, 1963).
27–29 *President's Tax Message along with Principal Statement,* May 3,
     1961, pp. 3 ff; reforms proposed: (1) pp. 10–11, (2) p. 9, (3) pp. 6 ff;
     (4) pp. 9, 26 ff.
29–30 Saving of $1.5 billion: Treasury Department press release, July 11,
     1962, p. 2.
     Eisenhower's similar idea: Henry Wallich, conversation with author.
     1962.
30–31 *Revenue Act of 1962,* Report of the Committee on Ways and Means,
     87 Cong., 2 Sess. (March 16, 1962): tax credit, pp. 7 ff; expense
     accounts, pp. 19 ff; withholding, pp. 84 ff.
30n. Senators Javits and Kerr: *Congressional Record,* Oct. 2, 1962, p. 20551.
31 *Questions and Answers to Explain* Proposed *Regulations Concerning
     Travel, Entertainment and Gift Expenses,* U.S. Treasury Department
     release, March 30, 1963, pp. 7, 8, 13.
31 Senator Gore: *Congressional Record,* Aug. 29, 1962, p. 17004. Reporting
     of dividends: All dividends of over $500 required to be reported, by
     Treasury decision, 1923. Minimum gradually reduced; by 1951 divi-
     dends of more than $10 must be reported. Treasury Department to
     author, Jan. 23, 1963.
31–32 *Revenue Act of 1962,* Senate Finance Committee Report, 87 Cong.,

page

2 Sess. (Aug. 16, 1962); deferred earnings, pp. 417–18; lobbying expenses, p. 23.

32 First Year Savings: *Survey of Current Business*, U.S. Dept. of Commerce, July 1963, p. 3.

32–33 *Economic Report of the President*, 1962, p. 26.

33 *Congressional Record:* Senator Clark (Sept. 6, 1962), pp. 17635–36; Dillon's letter (Sept. 6), p. 17653; Senator Carroll (Aug. 29), p. 17035.

33 President's statement: White House press release, Oct. 16, 1962.

34 Tax cuts: *President's 1963 Tax Message*, Feb. 6, 1963; compare table p. 55 with *The Right Kind of Tax Cut at the Right Time*, chart p. 38.

35 Business community: *Business Week*, Feb. 2, 1963.
President and bankers: *Washington Post*, Feb. 26, 1963.
Business leaders: *Membership List as of September 1, 1963*, the Business Committee for Tax Reduction (Washington).

35–36 Tax cuts: *1963 Tax Message*, table p. 24.

36 George T. Altman, "The Tax-Cut Mirage," *The Nation*, Feb. 16, 1963.
Another version: Statement of Douglas Dillon before House Ways and Means Committee, Aug. 12, 1963 (Washington).
Relief to Corporations: *1963 Tax Message*, p. 10; *Revenue Act*, 1962, Senate Finance Committee Report, pp. 11, 8.

36–37 Michigan Survey on shares: *1962 Tax Message*, pp. 261–62.

37 Robert J. Lampman, *The Share of Top Wealth-Holders in National Wealth, 1922–1956* (Princeton, 1962), p. 209.

38 Government spending: *1962 Supplement to Economic Indicators*, 87 Cong., 2 Sess., p. 430.

41 Walker: *Washington Post*, Oct. 15, 1962.

42 William James: *The American Pragmatists*, Milton R. Konvitz and G. Kennedy, eds. (New York, 1960), p. 44.

Chapter 3: The Visible Hand

43 President's remarks: *Washington Post*, Sept. 27, 1962.

45–46 Walter Adams and Horace M. Gray, *Monopoly in America* (New York, 1955), p. 173.

47 4¾ million: *Mergers and Superconcentration*, House, Select Committee on Small Business, 87 Cong. (Nov. 8, 1962), p. 6.
Norman R. Collins and Lee E. Preston, "The Size and Structure of the Largest Industrial Firms, 1909–1958," *American Economic Review*, Dec. 1961.

47–48 Top 4 manufacturers: *Concentration Ratios in Manufacturing Industry, 1958*, Census Bureau for Senate Subcommittee on Antitrust and Monopoly, 87 Cong., 2 Sess., Part I, pp. 43–46.

48 Concentrated industries: Carl Kaysen and Donald F. Turner, *Antitrust Policy; An Economic and Legal Analysis* (Cambridge, 1959), pp. 30–31.

page

49 Percent of value added: *Concentration Ratios,* 1958, p. 8, Table 1-A; fall and rise of concentration, pp. 43–46; increasing share of top firms, p. 8, Table 1-A.

Share of assets: Collins and Preston, "Largest Firms."

49–50 Mergers: *Merger Report,* 1962, pp. 9–13, 22–23, 34–44.

50 Textron: *Ibid.,* pp. 33, 104; *New York Times,* April 17, 1963.

51 Dominance maintained: *Concentration Ratios,* 1958, p. 9, Table 1-E.

53 Price fixing indictments: *Wall St. Journal,* April 3, 1963; *Business Week,* May 5, 1962; see also Chapter 4.

54 Steel crisis: Grant McConnell, *Steel and the Presidency,* 1962 (New York, 1963).

55–57 A. D. H. Kaplan, Joel B. Dirlam, Robert F. Lanzillotti, *Pricing in Big Business* (Washington, 1958), pp. 127 ff.

57 Bernard D. Nossiter, "The World of Gardiner Means," *New Republic,* May 7, 1962.

Steel prices, 1958: Gardiner C. Means, *Pricing Power and The Public Interest* (New York, 1962), p. 8.

58–59 Basic oxygen furnace: *Business Week,* Dec. 15, 1962; installed by U.S. Steel, *U.S. Steel Quarterly,* Nov. 1962; by Bethlehem, *Wall St. Journal,* Dec. 20, 1962; by Republic, *Wall St. Journal,* March 28, 1962; continuous casting: *Business Week,* March 16, 1963.

59 Brugler: Gilbert Burck, "The Private Strategy of Bethlehem Steel," *Fortune,* April 1962.

John Jewkes, "The Sources of Invention," *Lloyd's Bank Review,* Jan. 1958.

61 R. M. Blough, "My Side of the Steel Price Story," *Look,* Jan. 29, 1963.

Corporations finance from earnings: *President's 1963 Tax Message,* p. 270.

62–63 Harald Malmgren and Benjamin Caplan, "More than Keynes," *New Republic,* Dec. 1, 1962.

63 New investment: *Economic Indicators,* Sept. 1963, Joint Economic Committee, 88 Cong., 1 Sess., p. 9.

65 Unemployment: *Supplement to Economic Indicators,* 1962, *Historical Background,* Bureau of the Budget, 87 Cong., 2 Sess. (1962), p. 34.

Gardiner Means: *Administrative Inflation and Public Policy* (Washington, Anderson Kramer Associates, 1959), p. 15.

Means, *Pricing Power and the Public Interest,* Chapter 1.

Wholesale prices and unemployment: *Economic Indicators, Supplement,* 1962, pp. 34, 92.

67 Edward S. Mason, ed., *The Corporation in Modern Society* (Cambridge, 1959), p. 4.

68 Carl Kaysen, "The Corporation: How Much Power? What Scope?" in Mason, *The Corporation,* p. 99.

69–70 Robert F. Lanzillotti, "Pricing Objectives in Large Corporations," *American Economic Review,* Dec. 1958.

Adams and Gray, *Monopoly,* p. 71.

71–72 Kaysen and Turner, *Antitrust Policy,* pp. 45, 98.

Notes

Chapter 4: Of Consciences and Kings

page

77 Dean Horton: George Albert Smith, Jr., *Business, Society, and the Individual* (Homewood, Ill., 1962), p. 41.

77–78 Managerial creed: Francis T. Sutton and others, *The American Business Creed* (Cambridge, 1956), p. 263.

78 Owen Young: *ibid.*, p. 387.

79 Theodore L. Thau, "The Business Ethics Advisory Council," Annals, American Academy of Political and Social Science, Sept. 1962.

Editors of *Fortune* and Russell W. Davenport, *U.S.A.: The Permanent Revolution* (New York, 1951), pp. 68, 88.

David E. Lilienthal, *Big Business: A New Era* (New York, 1952), p. 27.

80 Adolph A. Berle, Jr., *The Twentieth Century Capitalist Revolution* (New York, 1954), Chapter 5, and p. 56.

Berle, Introduction to *The Corporation in Modern Society*, Edward S. Mason, ed. (Cambridge, 1959), p. xiii.

81 Berle, *Capitalist Revolution*, p. 174.

81–82 Harvard University Graduate School of Business Administration, *Register* (Cambridge, 1962), pp. 26–32, 44.

82–85 G. A. Smith, *Business, Society*, pp. 10, 12, 15; cases: pp. 107, 408, 168, 309; Eells: pp. 520, 752; Baumhart: pp. 42 ff.

85 Benjamin M. Selekman, "Cynicism and Managerial Morality," *Harvard Business Review*, Sept.–Oct. 1958.

Berle, *Capitalist Revolution*, p. 83.

85–87 General description of GE conspiracy: John Herling, *The Great Price Conspiracy* (Washington, 1962).

87–89 *Administered Prices; Hearings*, Senate Judiciary Subcommittee on Antitrust and Monopoly, 87 Cong., 1 Sess., Parts 27–28 (April 13–June 23, 1961), pp. 16939, 16936, 17206, 17284, 17256, 17670, 17700, 17711, 17761, 17116, 17117.

89 General Electric Legal Services, Interim Report, Dec. 14, 1960, p. 6.

89–90 General Electric, *1960 Annual Report*, p. 22.

90 Lilienthal, *Big Business*, p. 154.

90–91 Burger's plea: Herling, *Price Conspiracy*, pp. 209–11.

91 Ginn: *Administered Prices*, pp. 17070–071; Cordiner, pp. 17751–752.

92 Robert Lekachman, "Businessmen and their Rivals," *Annals*, Am. Acad. Pol. and Soc. Science, Sept. 1962.

92–93 Judge Ganey, Feb. 6, 1961: Herling, *Price Conspiracy*, p. 196.

93 McGovern and Motley: *Washington Post*, March 19, 1961.

94–95 Henry Ford II, "Business Ethics in 1961," address, Minneapolis, Minn., April 20, 1961.

Report of the 1961 Annual Meeting, General Electric.

96–97 Anderson: *New York Times*, Nov. 2, 1960.

97 Eisenhower: *New York Times*, Nov. 1, 1960.

West Germany: *New York Times*, Nov. 24, 1960.

97–98 Ford announcement: *New York Times*, Nov. 15, 1960.

98 Ford statement: Press release, Nov. 19, 1960.

page
 99 Ford England earnings: *Business Week*, Dec. 3, 1960.
 99 Anderson to Ford: *Business Week*, Dec. 10, 1960.
100 Gossett: G. A. Smith, *Business, Society*, p. 32.
    Editors of *Fortune, U.S.A. Revolution*, p. 78.
102 Option reform: *President's 1963 Tax Message*, Feb. 6, 1963, p. 21.
    Option debate: *Stock Options: Hearings*, Senate Finance Committee, 87 Cong., 1 Sess. (1961).
102–3 Romney and AMC stocks: Annual Stockholders Proxy Statements, 1962, 1960, 1959; Romney explains: *New York Times*, Jan. 6, Feb. 16, 17, 1960; *Time*, Feb. 29, 1960.
104 Theodore Levitt, "The Dangers of Social Responsibility," *Harvard Business Review*, Sept.–Oct. 1958.
104–5 Berle, *Capitalist Revolution*, pp. 169, 64.

Chapter 5: The Myth of Countervailing Power

107 David E. Lilienthal, *Big Business: A New Era* (New York, 1952), pp. 26, 33.
    John Kenneth Galbraith, *American Capitalism: The Concept of Countervailing Power* (Boston, 1952).
108–9 Biggest oil buyers: *Wall Street Journal*, Jan. 21, 1963.
109 George J. Stigler, "The Economist Plays with Blocs," *American Economic Review*, May, 1954.
110 Galbraith, *Am. Capitalism*, strong demand: pp. 131–32; unemployment: p. 196.
111 Gardiner C. Means, *Pricing Power and the Public Interest* (New York, 1962), p. 130.
    Steel strikes: *Collective Bargaining in the Basic Steel Industry*, U.S. Dept. of Labor (1961), pp. 253–54, 281–84.
111–12 Steel prices: Otto Eckstein and Gary Fromm, *Steel and the Postwar Inflation*, Joint Economic Committee Print, 86 Cong., 1 Sess., p. 34.
112–13 Maritime unions strike: *Washington Post*, July 16, 1961.
113–14 Unions stabilize industry: Garment Workers, M. P. Davies, *The World of David Dubinsky* (Cleveland, 1957), pp. 223–24; Hatters, *New York Times*, June 1, 1959, Jan. 24, 1961; United Mine Workers, N. Caldwell and G. S. Graham, "The Strange Romance Between John L. Lewis and Cyrus Eaton," *Harper's*, Dec. 1961; Teamsters, *Washington Post*, Aug. 6, 1961; Newspaper Reporters, *Guild Reporter*, Dec. 14, 1962.
114 Union lobbying: *Communications Workers of America News*, May, June, 1962; Clothing Workers, *The Advance*, March 15, April 15, 1961; *United Mine Workers Journal*, March 1, March 15, 1962.
115 Sidney Lens, *The Crisis of American Labor* (New York, 1959), p. 212.
    Diminishing employment areas: *Manpower Report of the President*, U.S. Dept. of Labor (March, 1963), pp. 74, 75, 164.
    Growing employment areas: *Manpower Report*, pp. 95 ff.

page

Proceedings of AFL–CIO 4th Convention, 1961 (Washington, 1961), Vol. I, p. 190.

116 White collar increase: *Manpower Report*, pp. 26, 165.

116–17 Geographical shift: *ibid.*, p. 23.

117 AFL–CIO *Proceedings*, Vol. I, p. 179.

Hoffa: *Washington Post*, Aug. 6, 1961.

117–18 Solomon Barkin, *The Decline of the Labor Movement* (Santa Barbara, Calif., 1961), p. 5.

118 C. Wright Mills, "The Labor Leaders and the Power Elite," in *Industrial Conflict*, Kornhauser, Dubin and Ross, eds. (New York, 1954), p. 148.

118–19 Barkin, *Labor Movement*, p. 5.

119 Dave Beck: *Final Report*, Part 3, Select Committee on Improper Activities in the Labor or Management Field, 86 Cong., 2 Sess., p. 63.

Reuther: Jack Stieber, *Governing the U.A.W.* (New York, 1962), p. 33.

AFL–CIO *Proceedings*, Vol I, pp. 202, 206.

120 Richard A. Lester, *As Unions Mature* (Princeton, 1958), pp. 27, 59.

Mills, "Labor Leaders," p. 147.

121 Arthur Kornhauser, Harold L. Sheppard, Albert J. Mayer, *When Labor Votes* (New York, 1956), p. 281.

Meany: Conversation of author with competent sources.

Barkin, *Labor Movement*, p. 65.

122 Galbraith, *Am. Capitalism*, p. 136.

122–23 Marver H. Bernstein, *Regulating Business by Independent Commission* (Princeton, 1955) pp. 87, 90.

123 Louis J. Hector, "Problems of the CAB and the Independent Regulatory Commissions," *Yale Law Journal*, May, 1960.

123–24 Morgan to Kennedy: Copy of resignation letter given to author.

124 James M. Landis, *Report on Regulatory Agencies to the President-Elect*, Senate Judiciary Committee (Dec. 1960), p. 71.

Samuel P. Huntington, *Clientalism: A Study in Administrative Politics*, Ph.D. Thesis, Harvard, 1950, pp. 378, 385.

Senators Aiken and Douglas: *Establishment of a Commission on Ethics in Government, Hearings*. Senate Committee on Labor and Public Welfare, 82 Cong., 1 Sess. (1951), pp. 213, 336–37.

125 Olney letter: Matthew Josephson, *The Politicos* (New York, 1938), p. 526.

Landis, *Regulatory Agencies*, pp. 35, 56.

126 *Report of the Antitrust Subcommittee on the Ocean Freight Industry*, House Judiciary Committee, 87 Cong., 2 Sess. (March 1, 1962), pp. 363, 397, 378, 362.

128 Merle Fainsod, Lincoln Gordon, Joseph Palamountain Jr., *Government and the American Economy* (New York, 1941), p. 663.

129 *The Budget of the United States Government*, 1964, p. 61.

Aerospace industry, electrical machinery: Merton J. Peck and Frederic M. Scherer, *The Weapons Acquisition Process: An Economic Analysis* (Boston, Harvard Graduate School of Business Administration, 1961), pp. 28, 129–30.

page

129–30 *Congressional Quarterly Almanac,* Vol. XVIII, 1962, p. 1021.

130–31 Don K. Price, "The Scientific Establishment," *Proceedings of the American Philosophical Society,* Vol. 106, No. 3.

131 Participants in administration: J. Stefan Dupré and W. Eric Gustafson, "Contracting for Defense: Private Firms and the Public Interest," *Political Science Quarterly,* June, 1962.
    McGuire cited: *ibid.*

131–32 *Report to the President on Government Contracting for Research and Development,* Bureau of the Budget (May, 1962), p. 8.

132 Concentration in defense contracts: Peck and Scherer, *Weapons Acquisition,* p. 117. *Background Material on Economic Aspects of Military Procurement and Supply,* Joint Economic Committee, 88 Cong., 1 Sess., March 1963, p. 9.

132–33 Federal contributions: *Reviews of Data on Research and Development,* National Science Foundation, NSF 62–9, April, 1962, p. 2; *Funds for Research and Development in Industry 1959,* NSF 62–3, Jan. 1962, pp. 10–11.

133 *Report of the Antitrust Subcommittee* (No. 5) *on Consent Decree Program of the Dept. of Justice,* 86 Cong., 1 Sess. (Jan. 30, 1959), pp. 31, 47, 63, 64–65.
    Earl Lathem, *Political Theories of Monopoly Power* (University of Maryland, College Park, Md. 1957), p. 6.

Chapter 6: The Split-Level Society

137 Gerard Piel, *Science in the Cause of Man* (New York, 1961), p. 288.
    Robert L. Heilbroner, in *Automation and Technological Change,* John T. Dunlop, ed., The American Assembly Series (Englewood Cliffs, N.J., 1962), p. 24.

138 Michael Harrington, *The Other America—Poverty in the United States* (New York, 1962), pp. 191, 30.
    Robert J. Lampman, "The Low Income Population and Economic Growth," *Study of Employment, Growth and Price Levels,* Joint Economic Committee, 86 Cong., 1 Sess. (Dec, 1959), pp. 4, 12.

139 Leon Keyserling (co-author), *Poverty and Deprivation in the U.S.,* Conference on Economic Progress (Washington, 1962), p. 2.
    Institute of Social Research, University of Michigan: James N. Morgan and others, *Income and Welfare in the United States* (New York, 1962), pp. 188–91.
    Private agencies: *Annual Price Survey and Family Budget Costs: Oct. 1959,* pp. 11–12.

139–40 Helen H. Lamale and Margaret S. Stotz, "The Interim City Worker's Family Budget," *Monthly Labor Review,* U.S. Dept. of Labor, August, 1960.

140 Keyserling, *Poverty and Deprivation,* p. 3.
    Lampman, *Low Income Population,* p. 35.

141 Harrington, *Other America,* p. 3.

Notes

page

Miners in Scranton: *Senate Report of the Special Committee on Unemployment Problems*, 86 Cong., 2 Sess. (March 3, 1960), p. 2.

141–43 *Unemployment Problems, Hearings*, Senate Special Committee, 86 Cong., 1 Sess. (Nov. 16–Dec. 14, 1959), parts 5–7: woman in Evansville, p. 2733; Chambers, p. 2385; Mercer Co., p. 2424; Fayette Co., p. 2539; skilled worker, Evansville, p. 2794; Miner, Letcher Co., p. 1994.

143 John Kenneth Galbraith, *The Affluent Society* (Boston, 1958), pp. 325–26.

143–44 Lampman, *Low Income Population*, pp. 25–28.

145 *Higher Unemployment Rates, 1957–1960*, Joint Economic Committee, Subcommittee on Economic Statistics, 87 Cong., 1 Sess., (Nov. 1961), pp. 4, 6. 1960–63 unemployment: *Economic Indicators*, Sept. 1963, Joint Economic Committee, 88 Cong., 1 Sess., p. 10. *Employment and Earnings*, U.S. Dept. of Labor, Mar. 1963, p. xii.

Peak months: *Employment and Earnings*, p. xii. November 1948 rate in *Monthly Report on the Labor Force*, January 1962, U.S. Dept. of Labor, p. S–4.

145–46 Recent history: *Employment and Earnings*, p. xii; *Economic Indicators*, Sept. 1963.

146 Annual report of the Council of Economic Advisers in *Economic Report of the President*, 1963, p. 39.

Piel, *Science in Cause of Man*, p. 290.

146–47 Galbraith, *Affluent Soc.*, pp. 140, 197, 300.

148 Chambers: *Unemployment Hearings* (Nov. 16–18, 1959), Part 6, p. 2386.

Additional job seekers: *Manpower Report of the President*, U.S. Dept. of Labor, March 1963, pp. 6, 90.

149 *Econ. Report of the President*, 1963, p. xiii.

150 Knowles study: *Higher Unemployment Rates*, pp. 78–79.

151–52 *Economic Report of the President on the Economic Situation and Outlook, Hearings*, Joint Economic Committee, 87 Cong., 1 Sess. (Jan. 1961), pp. 385–86; 378, 382.

152 Knowles and Kalachek: *Higher Unemployment Rates*, p. 79.

153 Kennedy: *New York Times*, Feb. 15, 1962.

Automation and Technological Change, Joint Economic Committee on the Economic Report, Subcommittee on Economic Stabilization, 84 Cong., 1 Sess. (Nov. 1955), p. 4.

Piel, *Science in Cause of Man*, p. 278.

154–55 BLS statistics: *Automation*, American Assembly, 1962, p. 117.

155 Knowles, *Higher Unemployment Rates*, p. 25.

156 Walter Buckingham in *New Views on Automation*, Joint Economic Committee, Subcommittee on Automation and Energy Resources, 86 Cong., 2 Sess. (1960), p. 32.

157 Henry M. Wriston: *Automation*, American Assembly, 1962, p. 172.

Elderly pensioner: *Health, Education and Welfare–Indicators*, U.S. Dept. of Health, Education and Welfare, May, 1963, p. 34.

158 U.S. and European growth rates: Robert J. Myers, *The Unemployment*

page

Problem: *What We Can Learn From European Experience*, Remarks,
Conference on Unemployment and the American Economy, University
of California, April 20, 1963.

158–60 Edward F. Denison, *The Sources of Economic Growth in the United
States and the Alternatives Before Us*, Committee for Economic Development, Jan. 1962, pp. 17, 21, 284–85.

159 If 4.5% had been maintained: Calculations by Paul Bradley.

161 Morgan and others, *Income and Welfare*, p. 3.

Chapter 7: The Two Half-Truths of Disarmament

166 Epigraph 1: *Replies of Governments*, Vol. 2 of *Economic and Social
Consequences of Disarmament*, UN Economic and Social Council
(New York, 1962), p. 175.

Epigraph 2: Charles J. Hitch and Roland N. McKean, *The Economics
of Defense in the Nuclear Age* (Cambridge, 1960), p. 70.

167 $120 billion: Report of the Secretary General, United Nations, Vol. 1 of
"Economic and Social Consequences of Disarmament," *Disarmament,
Its Politics and Economics*, Seymour Melman, ed. (Boston, 1962), p.
335; Blessing, p. 380.

168 Machinists' union: Fred J. Cook, *The Warfare State* (New York, 1962),
pp. 78–79. Hitch and McKean, *Economics of Defense*, p. 307.

Thomas C. Schelling, "Arms Control Will Not Cut Defense Costs,"
Harvard Business Review, March-April 1961.

$56 billion, 10% output: *Budget of the U.S. Government, 1964* (Jan.
17, 1963), pp. 61–62.

7.4 million in defense: *Economic Impacts of Disarmament*, U.S. Arms
Control and Disarmament Agency (Washington, 1962), p. 23.

Hitch and McKean, *Economics of Defense*, p. 69.

169 Jeremy Bentham, *The Theory of Legislation* (New York, 1931), p. 108.

170 Defense employment by industries and localities: *Economic Impacts of
Disarmament*, p. 3.

Defense employment by states: *Replies of Governments*, pp. 239, 290–92.
Multiplier: *Economic Impacts of Disarmament*, p. 8.

171 Unemployment, 1933–39: *Historical and Descriptive Supplement to Economic Indicators*, Joint Committee on the Economic Report, 83 Cong.,
1 Sess. (1952), p. 34.

Hitch and McKean, *Economics of Defense*, p. 81.

171–72 Unemployment and defense: Kenneth E. Boulding, "The Domestic
Implications of Arms Control," *Daedalus*, Fall 1960, Table I.

172 A. S. Goldberger, "Conversion: The Magnitude of the Task," *The
Nation*, March 28, 1959.

Emile Benoit, *Economic Adjustments to Disarmament*, part II of *Economic Factors Bearing Upon the Maintenance of Peace* (New York,
Inst. for International Order, 1961), p. 5.

10 million demobbed: *Economic Report of the President, 1947*, p. 1.

173 Emile Benoit and Kenneth E. Boulding, eds., *Disarmament and the
Economy* (New York, 1963), p. 290.

page

Tailspin Unemployment: *Employment and Earnings*, U.S. Dept. of Labor, March 1963, p. xi.

174 U.S. reply: *Replies of Governments*, p. 211.
Economic Report of the President, 1959, p. 13.

174–75 UN experts: "Econ. and Soc. Conseq. of Disarmament," in *Disarmament*, Melman, ed., p. 380.

177 $14 billion: *Reviews of Data on Research and Development*, National Science Foundation, NSF 62–32, Sept. 1962, p. 4.
Benoit, "Economic Adjustment to Disarmament," p. 14.

178 U.S. Arms Control and Disarmament Agency, general views: *Economic Impacts of Disarmament*.
Benoit, "The Economic Impact of Disarmament in the United States," in *Disarmament*, Melman, ed., p. 154.

179–80 UN consultants: "Econ. and Soc. Conseq. of Disarmament," in *Disarmament*, Melman, ed., pp. 366–67, 369–70, 374 ff.

180 U.S. reply: *Replies of Governments*, p. 202.
Arms Control Agency: *Economic Impacts of Disarmament*, pp. 2, 3.

180–81 William McChesney Martin: *Control and Reduction of Armaments, Hearings*: Senate Foreign Relations Committee, 85 Cong., 1 Sess. (March, 1957), part 13, pp. 1263–64.

181 Arms Control Agency: *Economic Impacts of Disarmament*, p. 2.

185 *Ibid.*, Tables I, III.

185–86 Richard C. Raymond, "Problems of Industrial Conversion," in *Disarmament*, Melman, ed., p. 159.

186 Wassily Leontief with Marvin Hoffenberg, "The Effects of Changes in Military and Nonmilitary Final Purchases on Output and Employment in U.S. Industries. Preliminary Input-Output Estimates," private paper, Jan. 24, 1961.

188 Arms Control Agency, *Economic Impacts of Disarmament*, pp. 7, 27.
Leontief and Hoffenberg, "The Economic Effects of Disarmament," *Scientific American*, April 1961.

188–89 "The ABC of 'Input-Output,'" *The Economist*, Sept. 19 and 26, 1953.

189 Recent history of input-output: Interview of author with Jack Alterman of Bureau of Labor Statistics, 1963.

Chapter 8: Planning and Freedom: A Modest Proposal

192 Gunnar Myrdal, *Beyond the Welfare State* (New Haven, 1960), pp. 1, 84.

192–93 *Scope and Methods of the Central Planning Bureau*, Central Planning Bureau (The Hague, August 1956), p. 18.

193 Ragnar Frisch, "Preface to the Oslo Channel Model," in *Europe's Future in Figures*, R. C. Geary, ed. (North Holland Pub. Co., Amsterdam, 1962), p. 258.
Manchester manufacturer: "Europe Charts its Business Future," *Business Week*, April 7, 1962.

page

193*n*–94*n* "German Miracle Under Debate," *Business Week*, May 11, 1963.

194 Stanislaw Wellisz, "Economic Planning in the Netherlands, France and Italy," *Journal of Political Economy*, June 1960.

John Sheahan, *Promotion and Control of Industry in Postwar France*, (Cambridge, 1963), p. 252.

198–201 Pierre Massé, "The Guiding Ideas behind French Planning," in *Economic Planning in France*, Political and Economic Planning, No. 454 (Aug. 1961).

201 French growth: Robert J. Myers, *The Unemployment Problem; What We can Learn from European Experience*, Remarks, Conference on Unemployment and the American Economy, University of California, April 20, 1963, Table II.

Charles P. Kindleberger, "The Postwar Resurgence of the French Economy," in *In Search of France*, Stanley Hoffman and others, (Cambridge, 1963), pp. 141, 157, 155.

202 Modernization Commissions: *World Economic Situation–Evaluation of Long-Term Economic Projections, Replies of Governments*, UN Economic and Social Council (June 1960), p. 61.

203 Targets: S. Wickham, *French Planning: Retrospect and Prospect*, MS., Jan. 1963, Table IV.

Descartes: *Economic Planning in France*, P.E.P., p. 228.

204 *Extension of Economic Planning*, Royal Norwegian Ministry of Finance, Govt. bill No. 1, Suppl. No. 1 (1962–63).

204–5 General description: Mark W. Leiserson, *Wages and Economic Control in Norway, 1945–57* (Cambridge, 1959).

205 Output: *Report on National Income*, Economic Planning Agency, Tokyo, 1963, pp. 3–5.

Growth: Myers, *Unemployment Problems*, Table II.

New Long-Range Economic Plan of Japan (1961–1970) *Doubling National Income Plan* (Japan Times Ltd., Tokyo, 1961), p. i.

H. Michael Sapir, *Japan, China, and the West* (National Planning Association, Washington, 1959), p. 34.

5-year plan targets: *Plan of Japan*, p. i.

205–6 Miyohie Shinohara, *Growth and Cycles in the Japanese Economy* (Kinokuniya Bookstore Co., Tokyo, 1962), p. 111.

206 Japanese Planning Agency described: Martin Bronfenbrenner, *Long Range Projections of the Japanese Economy, 1962–1975* (General Electric Co., Santa Barbara, Calif., 1958).

207 7.2 percent growth: *Plan of Japan*, p. 22.

Shigeto Tsuru, "Growth and Stability of the Postwar Japanese Economy," *American Economic Review*, May 1961.

Leon Hollerman, "Industrial Structure and Economic Planning in Japan," *Pacific Affairs*, Sept. 1960.

208 *Plan of Japan*, pp. 107, 36, 47, 72, 10.

210 Sheahan, *Industry in Postwar France*, p. 188.

211 Imports, Norway: Petter J. Bjerve, *Planning in Norway, 1947–1956* (North Holland Publishing Co. Amsterdam, 1959), p. 1.

Notes

page

Norwegian unions and industry, 1944: Leiserson, *Control in Norway*, p. 36.

212 Oil: *Wall Street Journal*, Dec. 19, 1962.

213 Kaiser Steel Corporation and United Steelworkers of America, *The Long Range Sharing Plan* (Fontana, Calif., 1962).

Railways: *National Mediation Board Agreement between Southern Pacific Co. and Brotherhood of Railway . . . Clerks, Handlers . . . Employees* (San Francisco, March 16, 1963), pp. 3–8.

214 "The Four Functions of Ned," *The Economist*, Feb. 23, 1963.

216–17 Sir Robert Shone: cited in "Discussion of the Effects of Planning," *Economic Planning in France*, p. 234.

219 Arthur F. Burns, *Some Reflections on the Employment Act*, Address, American Statistical Association, Minneapolis, Sept. 7, 1962.

219–20 Labor-Management Committee: Lloyd Ulman, *The Labor Policy of the Kennedy Administration*, MS, University of California (Berkeley, Calif. undated), p. 11.

220–21 Council of Economic Advisers "decisional model": *Washington Post*, Nov. 19, 1961; also, James Tobin to author, 1963.

Index